The Architecture of Gunnar Birkerts

The Architecture of
Gunnar Birkerts

Text by Kay Kaiser

The American Institute of Architects Press
Washington, D.C.

Centro Di
Florence, Italy

Design and production
by Centro Di della Edifimi srl, Florence
Printed in Italy by Conti Tipocolor, Florence
Typeset by Linograf, Florence
Photolitho by Mani Fotolito, Florence

92 91 90 89 7 6 5 4 3 2 1

Published by Centro Di della Edifimi srl,
Florence, Italy
ISBN 88-7038-172-2

Cover illustration: University of Iowa College of Law
Photo by Timothy Hursley

Contents

Gunnar Birkerts, Architect

Kay Kaiser

Introduction

Variability ensures evolution. Successful organisms adapt to different climatic conditions and even accommodate the toxic presence of man. But at the top of the endangered species list are those that exclusively eat the leaves of a tree that grows only at certain elevations.

Similar rules of life apply to architects. Many are undone by existing conditions, or merely by the presence of humans in their completed work. If the client doesn't finish them off before the thing is built, the user does so later.

Perhaps these architects cling too rigidly to a specific design signature or approach, or forget where they are or for whom they are designing. Others simply ignore their instincts. While they may rule the world for a time, all eventually join the legions of creatures that could not adapt.

The healthy evolution of architect Gunnar Birkerts seems guaranteed by the variability of his work and the flexibility of his response. His success has not narrowed his range. He meets the new client remarkably unencumbered by his own past solutions or by those of other architects.

These characteristics prompt structural engineer Leslie E. Robertson to include Birkerts among the "titanium people" he knows – those who have some special element, or spark, that makes them stronger than other individuals.

The personality the architect imparts to his buildings comes from his own complex character and background.

Initially he is as difficult to grasp as his architecture. A stranger overhearing a Birkerts conversation would not know whether he was an architect, an Eastern European poet enlivened by sudden freedom or a Jungian psychologist.

He is emphatic, yet accommodating and kind. Radical and traditional. Jocular and deadly serious. He is romantic, pragmatic, sentimental and always adroit.

Birkerts' combination of innocence and egotism charms rather than repels. He is at ease at the same table with barons and diplomats, but in other circumstances he retains the humor and sensibilities of a woodsman who is happiest in his own forest. In both realms he possesses a dignity that comes only from a thorough understanding and acceptance of self.

Similar qualities are in his architecture. One feels that this is an architect who works with everything he has in him.

It is ironic that Birkerts is known as a master of the grand architectural gesture – sometimes too grand and too strong, according to some critics – and as an expert designer of underground structures. The latter are all but invisible except for a glow from the depths at night.

He has tucked law libraries under the earth and then filled them with daylight at Cornell University in New York and on the Ann Arbor campus of the University of Michigan. He is currently working on several other subterranean structures where he respectfully does not compete with the existing architecture.

But there is another side. This is the same man who suspended a tall bank building from a cable and swung it over Minneapolis twenty years ago. Today, he plans a tower that will lean fifteen degrees beyond its foundation. Perhaps it is a reaction to being underground so often, or to architecture's recent condition, in which ornament carries the message rather than structure. Or maybe the tower is just what the client needed.

Some critics see only the emphatic side of Birkerts and accuse him of creating sculptural objects that ignore their contexts. They see the Federal Reserve Bank of Minneapolis and the Houston Contemporary Arts Museum and look no further.

Birkerts explains that it was his good fortune to design several structures intended for wide-open urban or suburban fields. They were settings without identifiable contexts that begged for sculptures people could inhabit.

Admittedly, his sense of contextuality isn't as literal as that of Robert Venturi's salt boxes or Robert A.M. Stern's Shingle Style in the Hamptons, but it is there.

It is of a more abstract variety. He draws upon the things you can't necessarily see on a site, but that you know subconsciously are there. His is a deeper vernacular that comes from the rock beneath the site and from the air above. It also springs from his own Latvian heritage, a body of influences not unlike the ones other architects from Scandinavian or Baltic countries brought to the American Midwest in the first three decades of this century. These influences allowed them to work within their personal contexts.

When Alvar Aalto wrote about his Finnish countryman, Eliel Saarinen, he regarded him as a bridge between his country's architectural heritage and the future. Saarinen found his design language in Finland, but transformed it to respond to larger architectural problems and the new culture in the United States.

Birkerts considers himself among the second wave of architectural émigrés who arrived in the United States just after World War II. Although his early experiences have mingled with those in the new country, it is possible to see traces of his Baltic background in everything he does. It is in the slopes and patterns of roofs, in the layered walls and in the ways he handles materials and light. These are the constants in his work.

Other architects have long admired his use of materials and respect for fine craftsmanship. There is a handcrafted quality and refinement about the work, whether the materials are wood, masonry, metals or new glass systems. Through tediously explicit detail drawings and construction supervision, the architect and his staff often extract Old World craftsmanship from contemporary crews.

There are those who would dismiss Birkerts as a stylist, but they have not looked beyond the surfaces to the order he brings to the interiors.

To him, light is a building material that is as tangible as brick. He treats it as a precious commodity, as do most people who come from far northern parts of the world. His architecture is defined by the balance of natural and artificial light. Walls split apart and become segmented in order to invite light inside through fins, scoops, oculi, reflectors and other innovations.

He insists, however, that each project is different because it is shaped by where it is, what it must do and who inhabits it. He has spent forty years honing that ability to produce the appropriate individual solution.

The emphatic formal geometry and austerity of the University Reformed Church in Ann Arbor, Michigan, were a response to the beliefs of the

The Federal Reserve Bank of Minneapolis under construction in 1971.
Photo: Schawang Studio.

followers of a transplanted Dutch religion. It is difficult to imagine that the same architect designed the Calvary Baptist Church in Detroit eleven years later. The gaiety of its forms and the exuberance in the common materials were, again, determined by the character of the congregation and the nature or the religion, as interpreted by the architect.

The fluid form of the Corning Museum of Glass grew from Birkerts' concept of the amorphous quality of molten glass. The structure's chromed, mirrored and glass block details fit the collection of transparent and often wildly reflective art it holds. But the architect took a different stance when he added to the formidable, pseudo-Renaissance Detroit Institute of Arts, originally designed in marble by Paul Cret. Mimicry was economically, technically and aesthetically out of the question, so he played with scale and delicate connections. His new granite surfaces softly reflected the Cret building wherever his addition came in contact with it.

A careful look reveals a lively diversity even within a Birkerts building. None sit motionless on the ground. Something within each of them pushes and pulls with such genuine muscle that everyone who stands near the structure knows that a well-exercised and romantic mind put it on paper.

Birkerts began as an architect in the 1950s when the imagery of the era was active and abstract, not static and pictorial. One sensed in the designs of Louis I. Kahn, Marcel Breuer, the Saarinens and others, the dynamic forces that had occurred in Mark Rothko paintings. When Marcel Duchamp's nude descended the staircase, one actually felt her move. The ornaments she wore on her ears were inconsequential; it was the sweep of her descent that mattered.

This concept is still with him. As in the work of other architects of this time, the drama in Birkerts' designs is bold and not overly adorned.

The Detroit Institute of Arts addition at first looks like a solid and carefully crafted bunker for art. Then one notices that its roof appears to float above its body. "This tells people that it is a modern building," Birkerts says. Similar play with gravity occurs nearby at the Fisher Administrative Center at the University of Detroit, founded by Jesuit priests. The building has the gray slate verticality of a monk, yet its top floor floats above the dark robes of its body. This building is also respectful of tradition while it declares its modernity.

One thinks of the mixture of oil and water.

"There were these conflicts," architectural historian Esther McCoy observed about Birkerts' work when she first met him in 1964. "Out of them arose the tensions which have always made his buildings so arresting."

The tensions are still there. They grow organically from the often contradictory needs of client and site which mix with the variegated elements in the architect's background and subconscious. A building emerges that is unmistakably his.

Attempts to further define what Birkerts does are as futile as writing on water.

The base of the underground University of Michigan Law School addition, Ann Arbor (completed in 1981).
Photo: Timothy Hursley.

Sharply drawn conclusions about style or design process recede beneath the surface before the sentence is complete.

He never was a rigid modernist, but he was educated by men for whom the Bauhaus was a place of employment, not a phase in architectural history. The International Style held no appeal for him. Contained in the name was a universal sameness which undermined his belief that the solution for each project must be specifically and individually formulated. Through an exercise of will, conviction and impatience with the merely popular, he remained almost untouched by postmodernism.

Birkerts is unlikely to join any future movement, although he may start one. Its only dogma would be to throw all dogma out the window, and start each project with this objective: free expression made with compassion toward the user and dedication to quality. The need to be avant-garde simply to bring about change is not a part of his process.

He will continue to practice his personal variety of architecture quietly in Birmingham, Michigan, a tree-lined suburb of Detroit set squarely in the American Midwest. He alternately describes the location as a confinement and as a place free of clamor, where he can hear his own heart beat.

His white two-story brick office is only a few miles from what once was Eero Saarinen's office, where Birkerts came to work from halfway around the world four decades ago. He chose Saarinen because he admired his vigorous and inventive approach to modernism. Birkerts' years of independent work since then have strengthened his conviction that modernism can be innovative and responsive.

It is unlikely that any press agent will ever package him for mass consumption, but he will continue to evolve in his own way as his reactions to the world and his new clients affect him.

And as this happens, structures will emerge that are as welcome in this confused architectural era as the sighting of a lighthouse at night in the fog.

His only gimmick is to have no gimmick that carries from one project to another.

It takes courage to work this way.

He has designed buildings that say, "Look at me, no one ever tried it this way before." The Federal Reserve Bank of Minneapolis said exactly that in 1968, and it won a place in the history of modern architecture.

There is more to Birkerts than games with gravity and the exquisite ways he manipulates a building's skin, however.

Those who know him best admire the many times he defends subtle decisions about material choices and form that reinforce his belief that architecture must be an art. These ideas are often presented in corporate board rooms where no amount of fabric wall covering softens the talk of budgets and timetables. He cajoles, educates, concedes where necessary and performs a kind of intellectual magic act.

He has won when the client realizes that the way light enters a building is an urgent factor along with the loading dock's location. The decision makers

Birkerts' 1975 proposal for the U.S. Embassy office building in Helsinki, Finland. Photo: Balthazar Korab.

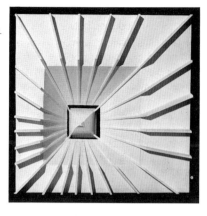

The atrium ceiling in the Freeman residence, shown here in model form, is representative of the structure and symbolism of the house. Photo: Balthazar Korab.

begin to think like the architect: the geological composition beneath the building actually may contain the clue to the type of stone used above ground. Mysteriously, their conversations turn to the satisfying quality of a fine piece of wood in a handrail set against white walls. Often they remember their reactions to trees, patterns and rhythms that they had not thought about for years.

"My methodology is not only what I put down on paper," Birkerts said in a recent interview. "Half of it is working with the minds of the people. I use everything I've got with clients – psychology, telepathy, everything. I like to synthesize everything, even the negative people on a building committee. I like to hear them and detune them in everyone's presence if they will allow it. In the end, everybody likes the solution and even the ones who were jumping on me are shaking my hand."

He disarms clients with the lyricism he was born with in Latvia, but they soon remember that the country is full of poets who also happen to be tenacious fighters for their principles.

Birkerts admits that following an individual course has not been easy. He has many scars delivered by clients who have been less adventurous or imaginative than he. He satirically, if not melodramatically, equates his wounds to those received by European gentlemen whose honor was upheld by duels, and their courage measured by the length and location of the sword's mark.

"You have to be strong to be an architect," Birkerts says. "You cannot turn your face. You have to take the beating and come back for more.

"The sting is only for a moment," he says, snapping his fingers. "Whatever they beat me with is insignificant in the total perspective of my life."

Since 1961 he has taught at the University of Michigan, Ann Arbor. He likes the challenge the students present. "The young minds are part of the *Zeitgeist*. They are the spirit of the times. I'm interested to hear what they think, what they say about the latest journal."

He tells his students about architects who found a personal approach to design, but who do not dominate the new magazines. Carlo Scarpa, Giovanni Michelucci and Ralph Erskine are among them.

In order to devote more time to his practice, Birkerts will no longer teach at the University of Michigan after 1990, but he is unlikely to completely sever his ties to architectural education. "If I know something, I want to give it out to somebody who needs it," Birkerts says. "Students know so little about real architecture and they get so little from professors who just teach. I can show them how to work for refinement.

"The art in architecture is to always shoot for the moon and have the wisdom to bring it back down to earth," he says.

The people in Birkerts' office help him do this. Principals Anthony Gholz and Kenneth Rohlfing have been with him for most of their professional lives.

Both are practical men who obviously have high regard for Birkerts, but who also are intermediaries between his concepts and the facts of the job.

Rohlfing cites Birkerts' former senior associate, the late Charles Fleckenstein, as a model for his own position: "He was almost Gunnar's opposite. Where Gunnar didn't connect with a client, Chuck did. That's why everything worked so well."

After decades of independent practice, he is at an age when many architects cling more and more tenaciously to their established precepts. But Birkerts' work continues to evolve. Ever since he designed the undulating glass walls of the Corning Museum of Glass more than ten years ago, he has been exploring forms that are more segmented, less orthogonal and more organically responsive to the natural shapes that surround the proposed structure. The activities inside the buildings determine the shape of their footprints as much as the will of the architect does.

"Maybe it takes maturity and a certain self-confidence to meander and let go," he says. The statement implies a growing flexibility, not a loss of control.

Heritage and Training

"I was born, more or less, under the same constellation as modern architecture, and very near to the birthday of the Bauhaus," Birkerts says.

He was born on January 17, 1925. His childhood years coincided with the country's brief period of independence between the two world wars. During that time, he could inhale the beauty of a country that was defined by the Baltic Sea, farms, pine forests, birch trees, meadows, lakes and a thousand rivers. Government-sponsored social programs made Latvia's standard of living the highest in Eastern Europe.

Latvia's symbols, mythology and literature shaped him before he could walk down the streets on his own. Indigenous and ancient folk songs, parables, riddles and sayings expressed the national spirit. Since the Soviet Union annexed the Baltic States, first in 1940, and again in 1944, this cultural heritage has become more precious.

A Latvian folk song tells of a fine silver rain falling on the night of the winter solstice: "God's silver coat is shining beyond the hill: make the fires bright in welcome!" Birkerts thinks in images remarkably similar to this. He also retains the laughter and "heavy, bear-like kindness" poet Czeslaw Milosz described in *The Captive Mind*. Milosz believed Latvians had stepped out of Peter Bruegel's country scenes.

His parents, Peteris and Merija Shop Birkerts, were among the scholars who collected and documented Latvia's cultural heritage in the early part of this century. Peteris was a writer, folklorist and philosopher. Merija was a folklorist, philologist and beloved teacher who remained in Latvia throughout the country's turmoil.

Birkerts inherited their verbal ability. Although his English is strongly accented, he often finds exactly the right word in that language, his third after Latvian and German. The symbols, wit and accessible metaphors that are in his

The Latvian landscape is dominated by trees, lakes and steeply sloped roofs.

Gunnar Birkerts' parents, Merija Shop Birkerts and Peteris Birkerts, in 1922.
Photo from Birkerts family archive.

architecture came from this exposure.

If only by osmosis, the interests of Birkerts' parents entered the boy and never left. Their books lined the rooms. It was his job to take them out on the balcony and dust them one by one.

Birkerts' first memories are of their house in Riga. When he shows a picture of it, he counts the five windows on the upper floor that belonged to the rooms his family occupied. The mature trees that filled the view with green leaves were important to him.

The father set many precedents for the son. Peteris Birkerts graduated from the Teacher's Seminary in 1902 and then became active in nationalist politics. His participation in the 1905 uprisings forced him to flee the country, first to Switzerland, and then to the United States, where his brother and two sisters had come earlier. Such extensive travel was unusual for the era.

With his family's help, Peteris studied law at Valparaiso University in Indiana and, after graduation, studied psychology and sociology at New York City's Columbia University.

He returned to Latvia in 1913, but fled the German invasion in 1918. He went to teach at Moscow's Social Science Academy and later at Smolensk. Merija and Peteris married in 1918 in Moscow and returned to Latvia in 1920. Together they taught at the Teacher's Institute in Riga where they collaborated on several books, now considered classics, that presented the folklore of the country.

Gunnar's interest in the psychological implications of design can be traced to his father. So can the fascination with the way the brain works in the creative process. The example of his father's courage in leaving the homeland in pursuit of freedom and opportunity is part of the reason why Gunnar's own plan to come to the United States seemed possible.

In Riga, he was exposed to a mixture of cultures which goes back centuries to the time when the city belonged to the Hanseatic League. Birkerts' experience was enriched by the varied European influences that lined the streets. Alvar Aalto wrote about the city in the publication *Kerberos* after a trip there in 1921:

"Now I must at once deny that I wish all people were architects or sculptors, but I do think an educated person, even a senior office clerk, should cross himself whenever he passes an old piece of limestone with a profile cut into it. In old Riga, you can see recklessly constructed towers, façades in blue and green, and at some workshop door or sausage shop, you can find a bunch of grapes so finely cut into the portal stone that they make you feel ridiculous.

"Riga seems to have been an international town for a long time. You can walk along alleys there which bear the stamp of Hansa merchant streets, you can find settings which take you back to the Sweden of Gustavus Adolphus. There are street views in the undisturbed Gothic style of the Teutonic Knights, and you can find palaces in such stylish High Renaissance, so aristocratic in their scale and materials, that your thoughts are taken straight to Italy's great Palladio. And if you know how to study what you see, someone will whisper in your ear the name of Haberland, Riga's master architect at the beginning of the 19th century. He is a man worth studying. And at the end of your rounds you slink into the Johanniskeller, the model of all peaceful taverns...."

(From Göran Schildt's *Alvar Aalto: The Early Years*)

Aalto ended his travel story by writing about the fragrance of plums that covered Riga in the morning mists. It had the effect of bringing forth "what is invisible to the human eye, my better self!" Aalto concluded.

These were the images with which Birkerts grew up. "It was layers and layers of real history," he says of Riga. "Parts were like Paris with two and three story buildings. And there was Art Nouveau and Heimatstil."

His high school, the first English gymnasium in Riga, was a dignified civic building next door to the British Embassy. "Being there in the heart of things made me feel like a citizen of Riga from the first day," he says.

The first day was in 1938. He does not remember how it was decided that he should enter the "realities" program – mathematics, physics, geometry, astronomy and the study of German and English – as opposed to the humanities. One can be certain that it was a carefully considered decision; education in Latvia was serious business.

Every year the seniors formally declared their future direction of study at university by mounting an exhibition of their work at the high school. He remembers it as such a big event that newspaper critics reviewed the show. A rendering of a modern building done by an older boy named Bernsons has stayed in Birkerts' memory forever. When he saw it at age thirteen, Birkerts decided to become an architect.

"That drawing made me tell myself that this was what I wanted to do. This was architecture, I belonged with it, and so it has been ever since."

It was like a flash fire, an intuitive experience. From that moment on, he drew buildings without any knowledge of perspective, but in a way that somehow expressed the modernism that was in the air at the time.

More than modernism was in the air, however. From 1940 to 1941, the first Soviet occupation meant the loss of democratic freedoms for Latvia. German forces claimed the country from 1941 until 1944, when the Baltic States again came under Soviet control.

In 1944 Birkerts departed for Noerdlingen, Bavaria, where he lived with August Grasis, a school chum from Riga, and his mother until the war

Gunnar Birkerts in his Riga home in 1927.
Photo from Birkerts family archive.

The roofscape of Riga, Latvia, a city of spires.

ended. He describes the town as a small and typically medieval place that had been a trading post on a Roman trail. It originally was built inside a protective wall, but had expanded toward a rail connection. After the urbane atmosphere of Riga, Noerdlingen must have seemed like the end of the world, a fact Birkerts alludes to in his notes.

He writes surrealistically about a place populated by men with bow legs and women with goiters "of unbelievable proportions." Only recently did he discover that the area had been hit by a meteor millions of years ago. He speculates about the connection between this event and the physical characteristics of the townspeople.

After World War II ended, Birkerts began the hunt for a university. He concentrated on Stuttgart because it was the closest to Noerdlingen. The occupational forces granted him a displaced persons status which allowed him to qualify for the foreign student quota. This put him in competition with Yugoslavians, Hungarians, Turks, Greeks and students of many other nationalities, all desperate to resume their lives.

While waiting for word from universities, he pursued a characteristically disciplined and specific plan. He studied German and English, because even then he hoped to leave Germany for the United States after establishing his academic credentials.

In December 1945, Birkerts was accepted at the Technische Hochschule in Stuttgart. He left Noerdlingen with his friend Grasis, who became his roommate in Stuttgart. Grasis later became an engineer and industrialist based in Kansas City, and is still his best friend.

Birkerts knew the school was his big chance. "Now I had the end of the rope, and from now on I had to do the pulling. According to my strengths, I would either make it or not," he says. He was twenty years old.

It was the first class after the war, and German students were competing for places more aggressively than foreigners. He remembers that they were older and fired by a great ambition to quickly build something, anything, out of the rubble.

"My interest was different. I wanted to know what the great Scandinavians and those who left for the United States had done outside Germany during the war."

The school was split between the Bauhaus faction and a traditional Heimatstil philosophy characterized by the work of Heinrich Tessenow and Paul Bonatz. The Bauhaus group on the faculty included the dean, Richard Doecker; Adolph Schneck; and painter Willi Baumeister. Drawing exercises were conducted next door at the Weissenhofsiedlung. Day after day the students drew the buildings of Mies van der Rohe, Le Corbusier, Walter Gropius, Hans Scharoun, Peter Behrens, J.J.P. Oud and many other European modern masters.

Birkerts winks at the memory. "It was Doecker's and Schneck's way of indoctrinating us," he said. "The people of Stuttgart thought the Weissenhofsiedlung looked like the Casbah."

He drew with the rest of them, but did not enter the intellectual debate between Schwabian regionalism and Bauhaus modernism. Even then, his only dogma was to follow no dogma. Those architects who explored a more flexible facet of modernism held a stronger appeal. Alvar Aalto, Erik Gunnar Asplund, Sven Markelius, Erich Mendelsohn and William Lescaze were among them.

His strongest personal influence at the Technische Hochschule was his thesis professor, Rolf Gutbrod, also an independent thinker. Birkerts says that Gutbrod liked the way he synthesized the influences of the designers he admired and worked with imagery the teacher had not seen before. The student admired the teacher as a professional role model, and at twenty-three, Birkerts also liked Gutbrod's sports car and the natty way he dressed. Architect as bon vivant was an appealing new concept for the young man.

He remembers Gutbrod's stories about Hans Scharoun and the mystical Rudolf Steiner, whose Waldorfschulen were intended to teach children his "anthroposophical" theories. They were "the path of knowledge to guide the Spiritual in the human being to the Spiritual in the Universe," Steiner wrote in 1925. "It arises as a need of the heart, of the life of feeling: and it can only be justified inasmuch as it can satisfy this inner need."

These ideas must have seemed as strange to young Birkerts as Steiner's unrestrained, sculptural buildings. But a part of his brain stored these images and concepts away for later, when he was ready for them. They were the first messages about how to escape the grid, which he would do for the first time on his own in Detroit's Lafayette Apartments in 1961.

Gutbrod's somewhat free-form, or mixed-form, architecture disturbed Birkerts. "At that time, I was extremely bothered by Gutbrod's solution for Stuttgart's Liederhalle because of its apparent lack of discipline and order. These were qualities that my young mind was trying to learn and look for – order and system as guidelines. In recent years I saw Liederhalle again and can trace its influence on St. Peter's Church in Columbus, Indiana."

The technical side of architecture at the Technische Hochschule was easier for Birkerts to absorb. He believes that the *Werklehre* (craft and technology) program provided a strong base for him. He learned how stone, metals and all other materials should go together. He remembers that recycling the war rubble was a very real activity. "You only had to pick it up and do something with it."

While still a student in Stuttgart, he went to the architectural library at the U.S. Information Agency, where he discovered the work of Eliel and Eero Saarinen. In the magazines were the General Motors Technical Center master plan, the first Brandeis University work and the Pharmacy Building at Drake University.

Birkerts was much more attracted to the work of Eero, the son, than to that of Eliel, the father. Years later, however, after he was working for Eero, others placed him philosophically closer to the father.

This house by Hans Scharoun in the Weissenhofsiedlung, built in 1927, showed Birkerts that there was a way to break out of the box of early modernism. "Scharoun was a freer spirit than the others," he says.

Birkerts visited Rudolph Steiner's Goetheanum II in Dornach, near Basel, Switzerland, in 1985. Its eccentricity, which puzzled him during his student days in Stuttgart, made more sense to him forty years later.

Kevin Roche believed that Birkerts "prized Eliel's lifestyle as a model over Eero's," as he wrote in the booklet honoring Birkerts' guest professorship at the University of Illinois at Urbana-Champaign in 1983. "Eliel represented the individual architect working alone in his studio, a traditional image, while Eero was the driving, brilliant pragmatist, herding a group of ambitious young architects through the intricacies of his own exceedingly complex approach to design.

"Gunnar was an individualist then, and over the years he has not changed," Roche wrote. Today, despite the involvement Birkerts' associates have in the office's projects, the original concept and the last word both come directly from him.

"I am often asked why I went to the Saarinens," Birkerts says. "In my effort to explain, I have always addressed the objectives, the similarities in working habits and other things, but by now I believe it was my destiny.

"The more I looked, the more I felt empathy with the Saarinen architecture. It was inventive and stimulating. And the best way I can describe my reaction was that I could hear it. It talked to me."

The Saarinen work was a tap on the shoulder similar to the one he had felt while standing in front of the student drawing in Riga. It was so strong that Birkerts never thought of applying at any other office in Europe or America. He chose Saarinen, and that was that. Now he had to find out whether Saarinen would choose him.

He graduated in early December of 1949 with a degree in architecture and engineering. On December 17, 1949, one month before his twenty-fifth birthday, his ship arrived in New York harbor after an eleven-day passage from Bremerhaven, Germany. He does not remember the name of the ship or any details of particular interest during the voyage. One senses that his mind was focused on the future.

His first reaction to the New York skyline? It looked just like a Hugh Ferriss rendering, he said at the time.

Today, it seems to Birkerts that until he left Germany, history determined what happened to him and what he did. In America, good things started to happen. He acknowledges that the hand of some unseen but no less tangible guide has been remarkably kind.

His American adventure could have ended at the immigration office, however. By law, every displaced person had to have a sponsor in this country, and Birkerts' sponsor, a North Dakota cattle rancher, never appeared. It could have been a long boat trip back to Germany had it not been for a Latvian friend he had met in Noerdlingen who vouched for him. The friend, Sylvia Zvirbulis, and Birkerts were married one year after his arrival.

In the beginning, he spent two weeks with Sylvia and her family in Princeton, New Jersey. Then he boarded a Greyhound bus for Bloomfield Hills, Michigan, and the office of Eero Saarinen. He had twenty dollars in his pocket and a letter of recommendation from Gutbrod.

When he arrived at the office on Long Lake Road, he had ten dollars left. He was told to come back between two and three o'clock in the morning. Saarinen kept peculiar working hours. Birkerts was admitted at three, but Eero told him there was no work at the moment because the General Motors Technical Center was on hold.

Saarinen had a friend visiting at the same odd hour – architect Minoru Yamasaki – who later designed the Lambert Airport at St. Louis and New York City's World Trade Center, among other buildings.

Yamasaki offered Birkerts a job in his St. Louis office. "I had no idea of the importance he would later have in my career. As I listened to his offer I was mentally confusing St. Louis with New Orleans – both places, I knew, had something to do with jazz – and since I didn't want to be that far from the East Coast, I declined the offer.

"It was another significant turn in a day that had been full of such turns," Birkerts wrote in the 1982 *Global Architecture* book about his work.

Armed with a recommendation from Saarinen, he headed for the Chicago offices of Perkins and Will the next day. He was hired by this large firm known primarily for school architecture.

"I knew I had no time to lose. I had to gain the knowledge and standard of performance of the other people in the office," he said of his first days at Perkins and Will. He mastered the Sweet's Catalogue quickly and studied working drawings every night to learn the American way of construction and detailing.

Apparently he absorbed this well, because hardly a year later he was sent to Rockford, Illinois, to supervise the design of a hospital. Then Saarinen's office called to get Birkerts back to Bloomfield Hills. The General Motors Technical Center job had started again.

When asked what it was that Perkins and Will or Saarinen saw in him, Birkerts at first says he doesn't know. "Maybe they liked the German education. At Eero's I was doing a lot of troubleshooting. I was doing the most difficult things there were to do, like going over things that had backfired, things that needed another look. They wanted me to be on top of it, in it, on it, and make sure that everything was buttoned up."

They probably recognized his perseverance. Without that quality, he could not have traveled so far with his drawings under his arm to appear on their doorstep at three o'clock in the morning.

"There is sometimes empathy between people," he explains.

Saarinen had come to this country from Finland in 1923 with his parents, Eliel and Loja. He knew about transplantation and the desire to make architecture

Eero Saarinen.
Photo: Balthazar Korab.

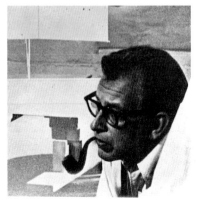

General Motors Technical Center in Warren, Michigan (1948-1956). Photo: Balthazar Korab.

in a country where many things were possible. Just after the war, the Saarinen staff was an enclave of recent émigrés from many countries: there was Willo von Moltke from Germany; Olaf Hammerstrom from Aalto's office in Finland; Spero Daltas, born in Minneapolis of Greek parentage; Anthony Lumsden from Australia; Cesar Pelli from Argentina; Mark Jaroszewicz from Poland; and many others.

Birkerts recalls the first time he met the noble von Moltke. He was the first to greet the young immigrant who had no appointment, nowhere to stay and a shaky command of English. Birkerts says that the courteous von Moltke shielded many people from Eero's often curt, irascible personality.

Journalists have described the Saarinen office as a stable of thoroughbreds. Birkerts remembers it as an intellectual roller derby where architectural philosophies and egos clashed. Saarinen was known as "The Bull." The turnover was tremendous: "Getting it done was what mattered," Birkerts says. "If you died on the drawing board, so what. Get the next one up."

He remembers Kevin Roche sitting motionless, holding his head. "I thought he was a prima donna who didn't have to work until I realized that he was thinking." Robert Venturi, fresh out of Princeton, was Birkerts' seat-mate. He, too, held his head a lot, claiming never to be satisfied with what he had done.

John Dinkeloo's boisterous verbosity was a revelation to the young man, accustomed to European decorum. The magic Hammerstrom and Charles Bassett made with Prismacolor pencils astounded Birkerts, as did the drawings of Eliel Saarinen that were still on the walls as reminders. Gunnar admits that he was never an accomplished renderer, "but I was a good thinker."

He kept his head low in this volatile atmosphere. "I was completely intimidated. Everyone was so eloquent. For me, it was like starting over again."

In the nearly five years with Saarinen, he worked on the General Motors Technical Center in Warren, Michigan; Concordia Senior College in Fort Wayne, Indiana; and the Milwaukee County War Memorial in Milwaukee, Wisconsin, for which he was the project architect.

Many critics believe that Birkerts' approach to architecture was totally established by his internship with Saarinen, but this was not the case. He came to Saarinen because their approaches matched. He was attracted by Eero's design and perhaps comforted in a strange land by the similar cultural and social background of Latvians and Finns. They shared the Scandinavian belief that buildings should be individual solutions to a given problem and made of materials that expressed their spirits in the most absolute ways.

After he had spent time in the Saarinen office, Birkerts began to have problems with Saarinen's methodology. Birkerts believed that the reliance on the model was a crutch that atrophied the imagination. "Eero was mysterious to me: slow, laboring, not trusting himself, and needing affirmations through endless explorations of a theme," he says. "He'd have a hundred models built, choose one, and then try it again."

The lag that occurred when a designer did not build the models bothered Birkerts because the creative process seemed to shift into the minds and hands of others. "In my office now, the designer builds his own models whether he likes it or not," he said. "Then the first-hand experience of the third dimension has a powerful effect on the design process."

He admits that it was difficult to leave Saarinen, but he wanted independence. In 1955, the same year Gunnar and Sylvia became citizens of the United States, they headed west with two small children, Sven Peter and Andra, to Milwaukee. It was not the land of opportunity. In fact, he calls it his year of disappointment.

That nothing went right in Milwaukee was not Birkerts' fault, says Donald Grieb, the architect with whom he was associated. The city was too conservative for the energetic modernism Birkerts brought with him from Michigan by way of Europe.

"I felt disgusted that we couldn't use Gunnar's wonderful ability to a greater advantage then," Grieb continued. "He could start with a brick and design the entire building from that. He was thinking about precast concrete members in unusual ways. He would take something that always was used flat down and put it upright. He was searching for something out in a distance."

Unfortunately, Grieb's bank client was not similarly motivated. Nearly every concept was rejected, only one of the two stories designed was built, and after Birkerts left town, a colonial façade was pasted over his work. "I'm happy Gunnar had the strength to get out," Grieb says.

He went back to Michigan in mid-1956 to work for Minoru Yamasaki in Birmingham. Birkerts believed Yamasaki possessed a spontaneous and intuitive understanding of the creative process that was like his own. As chief designer, Birkerts worked on the Reynolds Metals Building, the Educational Building at Wayne State University and the Dhahran Air Terminal.

During this time he designed two houses on his own, the Mequon House for the wooded suburbs of Milwaukee, and a prefabricated aluminum house intended to be shipped to the Virgin Islands. Both won Design Award Citations from *Progressive Architecture*, but neither was built. In 1960 he won a third citation for a swimming club, also unrealized. With other Yamasaki staff members, he won third place in a competition for the Belgian Congo Cultural Center. He also won a first prize in the Cantù, Italy, First International Furniture Competition in 1955. The honor held special significance for him since Alvar Aalto was on the jury.

These activities absorbed Birkerts' excess energy and mitigated his growing discomfort with Yamasaki's tortuously manipulated building surfaces. By day he served Yamasaki loyally, but by night he sought the direct expression of structure and simplicity of surfaces. When these midnight design activities no longer diminished his anxiety, he resorted to racing cars at a local track. He would have preferred to climb the simple walls of his own making.

Although he was named a principal in the reorganized Minoru Yamasaki & Associates in 1959, by the end of the year he left the firm along with principal Frank Straub and several junior designers. Together they became

Minoru Yamasaki's Reynolds Metals Regional Sales Office at Southfield, Michigan (1959).
Photo: Balthazar Korab.

Birkerts and Straub of Birmingham, Michigan.

"I had listened long enough," Birkerts says. "My apprenticeship was over. Now it was my turn to speak."

Straub was a fine project administrator and Birkerts was the designer. The partnership dissolved in 1963 because each man wanted different things from architecture.

The first independent projects of Birkerts and Straub were a reaction to the delicacy of Yamasaki and the technological detailing of Saarinen. The new work contained plain walls broken by directly articulated windows. The Schwartz summer residence in Northville, Michigan, won a First Honor Award from the American Institute of Architects in 1961. The Haley Funeral Home in Southfield, Michigan, was an exercise in Scandinavian form and window work. The exterior walls were pierced by narrow slit openings which become like bay windows that projected from the wall, pushing the glass away from the inner surface. They physically and psychologically separated the serene interior from the active world outside.

While the Yamasaki precast concrete filigree was absent in both projects, the Palladian symmetry characteristic of the office was retained. This tendency gradually shifted and responded to Birkerts' maturing method until a more organic asymmetry prevailed.

One of the first signs of this transformation was the partnership's first large-scale work, the Lafayette East Apartments near downtown Detroit. It was designed when Birkerts was thirty-six years old.

A decision to "slide" the two building halves produced more corner apartments and a feeling of added height and elegance. The plan was based on avoiding equally spaced columns. While this raised problems in the arrangement of apartments, it enabled the designer to keep columns out of inappropriate places. The two sides of the building are not identical, and the columns are staggered according to the apartment plan behind them.

"It is still organic," Birkerts said when he visited the building twenty-eight years later. He escaped the rigid Miesian grid through the irregularity in the building's exterior, and with its height and thinness. From the expressway that runs along the urban meadow of Lafayette's site, one can compare it to the nearby mid-rise and high-rise apartments designed by Mies van der Rohe. It takes only a moment to realize that even early in his career, Birkerts was searching for profoundly expressive forms within the parameters of the Modern Movement.

Saarinen's Milwaukee County War Memorial, completed in 1957.
Photo: Balthazar Korab.

Today, the walls of his small private office space are covered with sketches, sometimes three-deep. The College of Law at the University of Iowa appears in a construction photograph taken before its great round shell was encumbered by a roof. Next to this is a rough version of the dome for Duke University.

The ancient towers of San Gimignano are pinned up for inspiration, and a toy kaleidoscope ("it helps to oil the imagination") occupies a shelf along with important champagne corks, rocks, stainless steel window hardware and a miniature model of the papal throne he designed for Pope John Paul II's visit to the United States in 1987.

Among these things there is only one picture of a person. Close to where Birkerts sits at the telephone and tucked discreetly under a shelf, is a news photo clipped from a magazine. It's a smiling Alvar Aalto, and he's tipping his hat.

It is difficult for Birkerts to say that he has had a hero, but he has studied and respected Aalto since his student days. Although Birkerts made a study-trip to Finland in 1962, the two architects never met. "What would we have said?" He has no words to express his profound emotional connection to the man.

The reasons for the affinity are easy to understand. Latvia and Finland share the same sea and history. "Finland has a tremendous juxtaposition of horizontality and verticality and natural organic form," Birkerts wrote for *Architecture + Urbanism*'s Aalto publication in May 1983, seven years after Aalto's death.

"The lakes give one constant reference to the horizontal line and the dark pines and the light birch trees are pure verticality. The contours of the lakes give you all the free form you may wish. Aalto recalled these in his Savoy flower vase, not to mention his buildings. But Vuoksenniska Church for me is the greatest manifestation of Aalto's form language. There, Cartesian geometry merges with the natural free forms, generated by the interior functional or aesthetic requirements."

Birkerts used similar elements in the Corning Museum of Glass, the "Villa Ginny" house for the Fergusons, Camp Wildflecken, St. Peter's Lutheran Church and the Freeman residence. Aalto's light and volumes crept into the underground structures just as they danced around the mock courtrooms of the Iowa Law Library. It is, in fact, ridiculous to point to specific places where Aalto is found, because by now he is a part of Birkerts.

Look at almost any Birkerts design in plan and you see an Aalto vase. Instead of the ultimate flexible curved wall, Birkerts uses segmented sections because, he says, those are what Americans are willing to build.

"I doubt whether Fifth Avenue in New York or the Miraculous Mile in Chicago could call forth the best of Aalto," Birkerts wrote in *Progressive Architecture* in April 1977. "I say this even as I recognize that his sensitivity and design methodology could have responded with strength and purpose to the problems of urban America."

Later in the same article, he analyzed the elements in Aalto's work. "Simplicity and complexity, symbolism, metaphor, illusion, and contradiction, etc., are all accounted for. What fascinates and consoles me is that Aalto did not isolate and identify these in his conception. They seem to have taken their places naturally." He sees Aalto's architecture as the strongest

Alvar Aalto's Vuoksenniska Church at Imatra, Finland (1957-1959).

humanistic facet in the Modern Movement, a group in which he would like to be included.

Critic Sigfried Giedion believed that Aalto carried Finland with him wherever he went. Birkerts has done the same with Latvia, and it wasn't foolish baggage to bring to Michigan and other Midwestern states because the land is so similar.

Giedion observed that the Finn combined the technical and the primeval. "This same phenomenon appears in all the arts: out of forgotten strata of consciousness the elements of primitive man which are dormant in us are again brought to light, and at the same time unity is sought with the present day," he wrote in *Space, Time and Architecture*.

This is very close to what Birkerts has been trying to do. The intent and the images are subtle. The content from the past is never literal. In the era of postmodernism, when architecture displayed its historic and cultural origins so clearly, when all clients were put into an ornamented box, Birkerts' work often has been incomprehensible to critics.

His imagery does not come from the usual sources. There are no deep bows to any big chapter in architectural history. He has spent a lifetime exploring his own cultural history and the work of other architects who were born with similar inheritances.

Critics have been disturbed because they believe Birkerts is mixing northern mysticism with state-of-the-art surface technology. To drink from both cups is paradoxical, they feel.

Architectural historian Esther McCoy, however, realized early in Birkerts' career that a diverse set of influences might be advantageous. She came to this conclusion after spending time with the architect in his own surroundings.

In 1964 she was interviewing promising young American architects as part of a Ford Foundation grant to journalists. The results of her work were never published because "no one thought these young Turks were going anywhere," she said in 1989. Robert Venturi, Romaldo Giurgola and Cesar Pelli were also part of her project.

McCoy's assessment of Birkerts' potential was characteristically clear. She saw the "singleness of his purpose and the duality in his work."

She walked with him near his home in Bloomfield Hills on the grounds of Eliel Saarinen's Cranbrook Academy of Art. "I sensed in him some absolute need to refresh himself often in the presence of nature – not an American characteristic, and it served to remind me that he was born in Latvia.

"From that time on I began to pick out in his work an elegance of spirit and a poetry that was peculiarly northern in its crispness," she recalled in 1974 in a piece written for *Global Architecture*. Twenty-five years after their Cranbrook walk, McCoy said she remembered him most clearly there.

Birkerts told her that Aalto's Imatra church taught him that the rules for a structure's exterior could be different than those governing the interior. "This bit of wisdom made his design life a lot easier and enriched it as well," she wrote.

During the Ford Foundation work, she realized that classifying Birkerts' work was not an easy task. Although he ran his office "like any good, young dedicated architect, he did not have the compulsion, typical of one who had

The entry court at 1300 Lafayette East Apartments, Birkerts' first large commission in 1960.
Photo: Balthazar Korab.

spent ten years working in the offices of other architects, to establish at once a strong personal style with which he could be identified," McCoy wrote.

Nearly three decades later, he still has no compulsion to develop a style. While this has produced a rich and diverse body of work, critics don't know what to do with him. Baffled journalists turn to other architects whose more obvious consistency makes them easier to write about.

It frustrates Birkerts that writers prefer consistency over variability and subtlety. He remembers that Eero Saarinen was severely criticized for what many writers considered a lack of continuity in his work. He also remembers that several decades after Saarinen's death, they recanted, but that the lack of a full embrace hurt his short design life. "I wish he was still around so I could apologize," said Vincent Scully, a particularly fervent Saarinen detractor, twenty years after the architect was gone.

Anthony Lumsden, formerly with Saarinen, now chief of design for the Los Angeles office of Daniel, Mann, Johnson & Mendenhall, is also frustrated by the critics. He believes many prefer the acceptable refinement of horses to the quirky components in camels. Giraffes, rhinoceroses, rocks and trees are left out. "That denies a lot of life, doesn't it?" Lumsden asked.

"No one can explain me," Birkerts says. "Every building looks different. I am not postmodern or classical or strictly modern by everybody's standards."

He throws his hands up in the air and pretends to be irritated, but he is smiling. He knows that the qualities in his work that make analysis difficult are also its greatest strength.

The Work

Birkerts has described his architecture in three roughly decade-long phases.

The first, 1960-1970, represents his first independent work. It is defined by bold forms, space before structure, minimal detailing, stratified walls and daylight in interior spaces.

His college master plans from this period have a Metabolist nature that is related to the work done concurrently by Kenzo Tange and other Japanese architects who were exploring the synthesis of public and private spaces. Birkerts describes his Metabolist plans as systems that allow for expansion in a manner that is not unlike cell growth in an organism.

He calls the second phase, 1970-1980, the continuation. This was the period when he became intrigued with surface technology: metal and glass that expressed minimal sculptural forms and graphic quality.

The stairway at the University Reformed Church in Ann Arbor, Michigan, 1963. Photo: Balthazar Korab.

The current phase began in 1976 when he was appointed Architect-in-Residence at the American Academy in Rome. The phase is marked by the ongoing search for meaningful form and appropriate expression, he writes. His objective is to give a building personality with an expressive outer form generated by the organic functioning of the interior. The emphasis is still on interior daylight, the exploration of materials and physical and emotional comfort.

The lines between these categories are so fine that one wonders why they were established at all, except for the convenience of writers. The truth is that despite the variety in his work, Birkerts has been following an amazingly consistent path over the last forty years.

Therefore, it is much more worthwhile to look at the buildings individually than by decade. What concerned him in 1960 still motivates him today. His focus shifts among specific architectural concerns: daylighting of interior spaces, the layering of walls, materials that express the nature of the building, expressive geometries and a spiritual connection that links his understanding of the world with his client's.

How he arrived at the concepts is often as interesting as the architecture itself. Each building and each story is different, although they all have similar beginnings. The architect looked into the faces and psyches of his clients and began to formulate a solution that was right for them, at the time.

The University Reformed Church in Ann Arbor, Michigan, enters the mind quietly but deliberately. Many consider this building, designed in 1963, as one of his best because of the way he invited in the light. It defines the space.

He reaches for daylight indirectly through stiffening fins between the beams that work as light boxes. The beams reflect the light. But you are not aware of his method immediately. You sense mystery from the light as it is dispersed across the broad white walls. Other planes are seen in silhouette against the daylight.

Austere geometries in the concrete become soft, and the delicate layerings of light transform this into an emotionally moving, other-worldly place.

The use of wood where the building touches people further softens the church. But Birkerts sends out another subtle message: there is asymmetry at the altar in a building that at first seems rigidly symmetrical. This interplay between balance and imbalance is part of his organic view of the world which he shared with the Saarinens, particularly Eliel. There are many examples of it at the Cranbrook Academy of Art.

The architect brought light underground to the 60,000-square-foot addition to the University of Michigan Legal Research Building in 1974. The client did not want to obscure the questionable charm of the original Gothic-style library built in the 1920s.

Ironically, the buried library has more presence than most buildings that thrust their heads above ground. It is a riot of reflections, balconies and stairways brought three stories deep next to a V-shaped cleft in the earth. This was the first of many subterranean structures for which Birkerts now enjoys an international reputation.

Birkerts did not obliterate the beloved "mother building." Instead, he reflected it hundreds of times in the mirrored baffles placed along the bronze glass side of the trough. "You want Gothic? I'll give you Gothic," is the implied message from the fractured and dancing images. Although the effect is theatrical, it does connect the person inside to the view of the world above.

There is more operating here than reflected surface images, however. When one stands at the lowest level, at the base of the angled limestone wall that forms one side of the trough, one feels an overwhelming power of structure. "It is like the pyramids," Birkerts says with only slight embarrassment at the drama of the statement. "You are at the energy source."

The limestone wall reflects and diffuses the light coming through the glass wall. A triangular opening reaches for light at the back of the building. The result is the sense that light is coming from two sides. This is an act of magic in an underground structure.

Calvary Baptist Church in Detroit, designed in 1974, also plays with mirrors. Birkerts covered the immense front wall of the sanctuary with mirror to reflect the image of everyone participating in the service.

Did the architect go too far? When you see pictures of Calvary, one wonders whether the mirrors are any more than an architectural stunt. The doubt ends when one attends a service here.

Birkerts realized early on that this predominantly black congregation was energetic and that its members were profoundly aware that their faith was reaffirmed primarily by each other. The architect wanted to reflect that, too. And he did.

Through the mirror, you are brought in close visual contact with everyone there. Because of distances from the mirror and its incline, the minister becomes a minor element in the reflected image and the congregation dominates. The baptismal font runs like the River Jordan through the entire front of the picture with the congregation supportively behind. Since this is the core of the religion, its reflected presence is absolutely correct. The blues, greens and patches of wood reflected in the mirror are symbols of life.

On the Sunday this observer visited Calvary, many people wore the colors of the church, which speaks of the power of architectural suggestion and their oneness with the building.

The light inside is even and soft, exactly what one would expect from Birkerts. The tall slits of window openings provide just enough of a view of trees and sky to orient people to the outside. Any wider view of this area near Detroit's core would be detrimental to the uplifting experience church is supposed to be.

That the architect and his staff took pictures of everyone in the congregation and glued them into the original presentation model illustrates that they understood who the church was for.

This building is undeniably a roof-dominant sculpture. The design emerged because the congregation wanted a church unlike any other. It wanted to celebrate common materials and the forward-looking modernity Birkerts' architecture promised.

Birkerts had a client with a different need in 1970 at the Houston, Texas, Contemporary Arts Museum. Sebastian "Lefty" Adler, the museum director involved in the design process, wanted to be on the cutting edge. The architect responded by sheathing the building in stainless steel as cool and sharp as a knife blade. The clear span space inside allowed the museum to invite artists who wanted to shoot paint from cannons or start fires if they were so inclined.

In Corning, New York, the architect designed a fire station that is so red and shiny, so full of American fire truck imagery, that the building seems only temporarily parked. It is ready to speed off amid a cacophony of lights, screaming sirens, rattles and clangs. The building, designed in 1973, is triangular, but Birkerts didn't know this shape was an ancient symbol for fire until after the firehouse was built.

In 1974, the design of the IBM office building in Southfield, Michigan, transformed the architect into an inventor.

Although the 14-story structure's wall area was only 20 percent glass, the two-foot-high sloping glass ribbons brought light and views inside while saving energy. Daylight enters and is diffused by a curved, matte-finished stainless steel reflector placed on the lower edge of the window ribbons. Light bounces up and off this element to a light colored aluminum reflector mounted on the upper edge of the ribbons. The result is naturally lighted floor space even in the deepest recesses.

The architect balanced daylight with fluorescent lighting strips that run around the edges of the ceilings and meet the interior reflectors. On dark days, the artificial lighting system illuminates the interior reflector and the walls into which the windows are set. Because of these features the openings do not appear as narrow strips against a dark wall.

And by optical magic, the view through the windows seems greater than one would expect from the narrow openings. His inspiration for the arrangement came while looking out the window of a 747 jet.

The thick exterior wall required to accommodate these scoops and reflectors added to the building's energy efficiency. The silver aluminum on the south and west exterior and the charcoal black on the north and east further enhanced the efficiency and became a visual symbol of conservation.

Yet Birkerts can divest himself of technological baggage and get back to basics in a hurry. He has nestled houses and small office buildings into ravines with a naturalness equaled only by animals whose genetic inheritance directed them to build in the forest. The 1989 Holtzman & Silverman office in Southfield, Michigan, is a sophisticated example.

Square oak timbers and a roof of tree limbs define the outdoor worship space for a group of fellow Latvians at Three Rivers, Michigan. Designed in 1972, it is as close to a natural opening in the woods as is possible when an architect is called to rearrange the world.

The school Birkerts designed in Columbus, Indiana, fits into the neighborhood seamlessly. Lincoln Elementary School, designed in 1965, is a square inside a circle. The basic geometries are simple, but within them are the layerings of light and walls that are characteristically Birkerts.

The square structure was dropped one story below street level and the circle was formed by bermed earth to further minimize the mass of the building. Trees were planted along the ring to make what the architect calls a "green wall."

"There are circumstances in which buildings must serve functions without being visually assertive, or, rather, visually competitive with the rest of the urban fabric. Sometimes they are appreciated for their tact and modesty," Birkerts wrote in a description of the project in *Global Architecture* in 1982.

The secondary benefit of the raised berms is that they prevent balls from rolling into the street and reduce the risk of children running into traffic.

The center of the square plan is the multi-purpose room. This is surrounded by a ring of balcony-like corridors and by an outer ring of classrooms. The second floor corridor and the walls of the multi-purpose room do not touch. The games and events conducted there can be viewed from the upper corridor through sloped glass panels. Light comes in on the perimeter of the central space and does double duty because it illuminates the upper and lower corridors.

"This follows one of my key lighting principles, that light is to be reflected, deflected and otherwise 'borrowed' into spaces that lack direct access," Birkerts explained.

Windows on the exterior walls were positioned to give light to two rooms simultaneously. The side walls reflect this light into other areas. The young students are aware of the outside world, but are not distracted by a direct view.

The school was built during energy-conscious times. The efficiency of the enclosing wall was important in controlling heat gain and loss.

The school is more than a technical achievement, however. The interior is really a giant example of tight cabinet-making. It reminds one that Birkerts spent his off-hours at Yamasaki's office designing furniture and refining the ways two pieces of wood could fit together.

On another level of thought, the wood and detailing of the sloped interior wall make the interior feel like it is protected by a ship's solid bulkhead. On a visit to Columbus twenty years into the building's life, he patted the surface and called it the "Mayflower" – revealing a slightly confused understanding of America's nautical and historical legends. The facts are immaterial; it is the pioneering spirit of the endeavors that sticks in his mind.

The Dance Instructional Facility at the State University of New York in Purchase had an equally technical program for a very different use. The architect intensively researched other dance facilities and found that most were studios, renovations or mixed-use buildings. There was no direct precedent for a new school of dance. The design team met with the faculty of other schools to discover what they would ask for if they could start from scratch.

The dean of the New York school, William Bales, envisioned dancers moving outdoors in the sun, free of any enclosure. To Birkerts' mind, the dean was describing a garden. The architect took this as his metaphor and combined it with the practical elements the dancers needed.

The space needed to provide a strong sense of direction that would allow the dancers to maintain their orientation. Again, Birkerts did this with light. The tilted glass wall admits light most strongly from one side. It reaches for the sun just as the dancers inside reach for an ideal airborne state.

The site was restrictively narrow, but the architect's long, attenuated corridors became symbols of grace.

At the five-story University of Iowa College of Law, the circle – architecture's purest form – defined the building. The architect believed the study of law and justice deserved a form that expressed perfection, integrity and clarity.

Some people see references to the silos which are both symbolically and economically important to Iowa. Still others see Birkerts' abstracted dome as an update of the gold leaf dome of the venerable state capitol building across the Iowa River where the College of Law was formerly housed. Some, who know how rigorous a legal education is, interpret the new structure as a cloistered monastery.

Birkerts stayed with the symbol of the circle because it was dictated by conditions of the site and program. There was no orthogonal axis on the hilltop – only the river on one side, a curving highway on another two sides and a tree-filled ravine on the other. These elements called for a building that slipped into the site without hard edges.

The usually unexpandable circle worked for this school because the size of the student body will remain constant from year to year. In the library's current configuration, it can hold 800,000 volumes, but with the addition of compact storage systems on the ground floor, one million volumes could be accommodated.

The irregularities cut into the circle do more than simply vary the form. They allow more light into the building, and they saved the life of a tree that was there first.

Above the library are many faculty offices that receive daylight from the front, under ceilings covered by aluminum hoods that curve down to the roof.

The woodwork in Lincoln Elementary School suggests ship joinery.
Photo: Keiichi Miyashita.

The horizontal details of the limestone walls, the way they open to several types of windows and the quality in the metal work are good examples of the precision and refinement of which Birkerts' admirers speak. The silver-colored aluminum dome and the turrets housing the fire stairs have a machined quality, yet they are romantic.

The layerings of planes in this building allowed the architect to bounce light from many directions. Curiously, the school's auditorium/courtroom area and the architect's church work evoke a similar spiritual feeling. It comes from the combination of diffused and sparkling light from unseen sources. The architect-designed oak furniture and the lath work at the judge's bench add to this feeling.

These buildings illustrate aspects of the individual approaches Birkerts has taken. Squares, circles and triangles were all enlivened by light in ways that suited the inside life of the building.

It may be significant to an understanding of Birkerts that he grew to specialize in churches, schools and libraries. Nurturing the soul is a mandatory part of the program in these buildings. They are resonant because of their subtlety.

Leslie E. Robertson, the structural engineer who has worked with Birkerts for more than twenty years, applauds his flexibility.

"When people start constricting their thoughts into neat, pure, clean lines there are difficulties. You must be flexible," Robertson said. "The quest for completeness of thought many Germanic architects have is often detrimental to the quality of the architecture and almost always to the quality of the engineering. Many have a rigidity which Gunnar has escaped."

The respected New York engineer delights in the variety. "He has a very fertile imagination with clarity of thought, but he doesn't let that clarity bear down on him to the point where he can't bring elegance, lightness and fun to the architecture," Robertson said.

He was the engineer with whom Birkerts consulted for the Federal Reserve Bank in Minneapolis. While Robertson sees swashbuckler characteristics in the architect, he quickly adds that there is clear logic in operation when he stands at the end of the gangplank. "The work Gunnar does is based soundly within the technology. I don't think any of the buildings we've done with him are risky," said the engineer, who climbs mountains and races cars in his off-hours.

"The clients know I am an innovator before they interview me," says Birkerts. "If they don't have the nerve, they don't take me."

His intent to surpass the previous is never far below the surface.

The architect steps out on the tightrope and presents a perfectly logical explanation for hovering over the crowd. His reason for being there is so convincing, so rooted in practicality and concern for the user, that his best clients walk right out on the rope behind him.

When the conditions are right, Birkerts' architecture performs a triple somersault, and he lands his place solidly in architectural history.

This is what happened at the catenary Federal Reserve Bank in Minneapolis. At its heart is a tightrope, of sorts. The building contains so many of the architect's strengths and vulnerabilities, that it deserves a lengthy look.

The reason behind the curved cable suspending the bank from two supports is that vast amounts of clear space were needed below ground for the bank's high-security work. But the building also needed eleven stories of office space above ground. The office space could not spread out horizontally because of land coverage restrictions from the city's redevelopment agency.

Without the catenary, the building could not have contained what it needed and still stand.

"After working with the building program, it became clear that the building had a split personality. On one hand the spaces wanted to be opaque and impregnable, and on the other, they wanted to be transparent and communicative. The first, subterranean, and the second, airborne," he wrote in the 1982 Global Architecture monograph.

The architect becomes uncomfortable when he is called a daredevil in connection with the bank. His response is that of an engineer. He speaks of the tension of vertical structural members below the catenary. The members above are in compression. Floor structure spans between the structural wall planes. Counteracting the catenary forces is the thirty-foot-deep truss which acts as a compression member, and the space between the two trusses encloses mechanical equipment.

Yet when he talks about the building's metaphors, he becomes airborne.

He views the structure and plaza as a symbolic expression of the geological formations of the region. "One can think of it as a granite mountain that has been shaved down to form the sloped plateau...." The imagery was intended to symbolize the spirit of the people who settled the area and endured the raw weather and land. At other times he thinks of the bank as a gateway to this northern part of the world.

He was praised worldwide for synthesizing a contradictory program in a breathtakingly inventive way. Many believed it was an act of genius to allow the bank's skin to communicate the structure and the enclosure simultaneously through a change in plane.

Birkerts clearly enjoys the praise. "Other architects asked themselves why the hell they didn't do it first," he says.

Charles Jencks thought too many architects were grabbing monumental minimalist images in the late 1960s and early 1970s, and wrote so in a chapter of his Architecture Today, titled "Slick-Tech: The Rhetoric of Corporate Proficiency."

He complained of giantism, and to his eye, the surface components of the bank formed only a giant M – which stood for Minneapolis. He saw the great gateway as blocked: a "minimalist triumphal arch turned upside down and filled in the middle." He intimated that Birkerts' metaphors were malapropisms which European émigrés were likely to make.

But Jencks also gives left-handed praise. He wrote that the building brought a sense of stability and permanence to a transitional urban area where parking lots provided the only definition.

Years later, the architect can take solace in knowing that the bank is immediately identifiable to the lay public and professional observers. In the same day, a Minneapolis school girl and Allan Temko, the perceptive San Francisco architecture critic, both described the Federal Reserve Bank without words. They simply imitated the sweep of the catenary arch with their hands.

Birkerts admits that the plaza is not the best. It's too hot in summer, and the winter ice makes the sloping surface treacherous. Ropes for hand-holds are strung to avoid lawsuits.

But he made a building no one can forget.

Birkerts cannot forget Hugh Galusha, the president of the bank, who selected him as its architect. He was an accountant by training and had never been the client for a major architectural project. He interviewed several architects, all "big-shooters," as Birkerts recalls, but Galusha chose Birkerts, the "little guy," at the time with a staff of only six people.

"We had this enormous empathy," he recalls. "He sensed me. Galusha said later that I got the job because of my background. He thought that I was a survivor. He believed I would do what I said and that I would finish it."

Galusha also told Birkerts of the moment when the decision was made to have him design the bank. They had traveled to Ann Arbor, Michigan, to see the University Reformed Church, one of Birkerts' few built works at the time. "I confessed everything that was wrong with the church," the architect says. "We had concrete problems. We poured when it was too cold and it boiled over the insulated forms... But Galusha said he knew I was the one. It was important to him that I could admit failure.

"He gave me absolute trust even though I didn't have a track record," Birkerts says. "It was a $36 million job in 1968. Now it would be $80 million. He batted for me even though he didn't know much about architecture, and he got things through the board of directors. It wasn't based on a drawing or a model, but sometimes only on my word. There was this trust. And he saw to it that this was a total job – we worked out the details and the interiors."

Galusha died while the bank was under construction. He was separated from his companions in a snowmobile outing and froze to death. The tragedy had a profound effect on Birkerts. He continues to feel the loss of the man as a friend, and what he represents to architecture: the rare client with the will to produce a great building.

"If you have a building that has a need, a particular charge to do something; if there is a soul somewhere in the program ... this is the biggest challenge," Birkerts said to the students of the University of Illinois at Urbana-Champaign in 1983. It seems that, more often than not, the soul he mentions belongs to an extraordinary individual.

He began to work with Thomas Buechner, then the director of collections for the Corning Glass Center in Corning, New York, in 1971.

He was the man entrusted by the board to build the museum. There was no board of directors for the architect to face over every decision, and Buechner was in charge of installing the collection. Every object's location was planned by the man who knew the collection best.

"All my one-to-one clients have been good," Birkerts said. "And Tom Buechner was very good. He is a painter and the former director of the Brooklyn Museum. And he knew what the Corning Museum had to do."

First the structure had to be raised off the ground; a severe flood in 1973 had proved that the site was, indeed, a floodplain. Then the 20,000 objects in the collection had to be organized in a way that naturally led the visitor through the exhibit.

The solution was to place Corning's most valued treasures at the heart of the structure in display cases Buechner called "masterpiece columns." The visitor moves in a circular pattern toward the perimeters of the building, where displays of increasingly specific interest are located. If the visitors' interests are prompted, they go into the petal-shaped galleries where the world history of glass is presented. If the guests are drawn only by the masterpieces at the center, they look at those and find their way out easily, without adding to congestion.

Birkerts calls this organic design. The uses of the interior space pull the building into its shape. Buechner calls it brilliant. "Gunnar's conceptual abilities seemed so imaginative, and his attention to detail was equally creative. He was tenacious in approach and always involved with light. The periscope window in the galleries allowed people to be aware of the factories outside. They could see where the glass came from," he says.

Buechner remembers many dinners and hours of talk with Birkerts. It was clearly a relationship between two artists. "I hope that I get to build something with Birkerts again," he says more than a decade after they worked together.

He feels this way despite the problems that developed in the museum later. Holes in the vapor barrier allowed the moisture generated from the museum's humidifying system to condense at the face of the curtain wall. In winter, the building wore a necklace of icicles.

The situation has since been corrected. Who was at fault is immaterial at this point, but it does bring into play another important aspect of Birkerts' work. Despite his experimentation with new materials and systems, he has not encountered a higher failure rate than that experienced by architects who stayed with traditional, proven methods.

His risks are carefully calculated: he arms himself with a full understanding of materials, engineering and the qualitative reassurance of manufacturers. The architect listens to his engineering consultants who, in turn, believe he has a sound intuition about structure. But when available technology doesn't stretch to match his vision, he is philosophic. While unpleasant, an occasional material or installation problem is the price of practicing architecture today. Waiting the ten or fifteen years some products or systems require to be proven is not worth the loss of invention, despite these litigious times.

Thomas B. Monaghan, the founder of Domino's Pizza, Inc., was the most difficult client Birkerts ever had to accommodate. The difficulty increased logarithmically because Monaghan's already strong personality was enhanced by his zealous love for the spirit of Frank Lloyd Wright, perhaps the architect with the most carefully designed professional personality and philosophy America has ever produced.

Monaghan knew exactly what he wanted for his one-million square-foot corporate headquarters in Ann Arbor, Michigan. Not only did he want Wrightian horizontality, brick, deep overhangs and dominant roofs; he had a specific design in mind. He came to Birkerts late in 1983 asking for an enlarged version of the never-built McCormick house, a commission in Lake Forest, Illinois, that Wright lost in 1907.

Monaghan wanted to be the patron who set the record straight by building the design the architect was not allowed to.

Birkerts recognized the sincerity of this prairie Medici. He also knew that Monaghan was unschooled in architecture but was highly intuitive. Both qualities appealed to the teacher in Birkerts.

The architect sensed that Monaghan "had not read the whole book on Wright." He patiently and respectfully proceeded to teach him about the deeper nature of organic architecture, incorporating some original Birkerts philosophy.

But the sessions were more difficult than the architect expected. "Monaghan's Trojan Horse – Frank Lloyd Wright – was so strong and so good that he was hard to fight," he says.

Looking toward the skylight and mirror details in the lobby of the Corning Museum of Glass, completed in 1980.

His first master plan, a circular formation, was rejected because it was too much Birkerts and not enough Wright. Monaghan thought it was too high-tech.

The second attempt was full of McCormick house, but the Birkerts magic had begun to take effect. While Monaghan was looking at the model that contained everything he wanted, his eyes were drawn to a drawing on the wall that involved seven parallel "tracks" that raced across the land. "I was getting irritated by then. Why is he doing these other things that are nothing like the McCormick house? Yet I liked them. And he wasn't even showing them to me," Monaghan says.

"Later he brought out a model of the drawing and I was more intrigued. But it was like asking me to change religions. McCormick was something I had been thinking about for so many years, and now he's coming up with something better."

Monaghan spent four tortuous days wrestling with his faithfulness to Wright before saying yes to the tracks. It was the right decision. The design can be expanded to contain any change in warehouse, office, laboratory or public space the corporation may need.

Today, the more than half-mile-long complex flies across the land like a freight train. It dives into bermed earth at the appropriate places and is so horizontally dynamic that it makes the heart skip a beat. Monaghan smiles because his business functions well within the complex, yet it still looks somewhat like a prairie house. Birkerts is satisfied because the design is his own. He withstands the criticism that the design is not quite Wright and not quite Birkerts, either.

"I am not known for bending out of shape for money or other people's principles," he said. "My quest was to not get swayed to where I lost my identity. As long as it was fifty-one percent me and forty-nine percent Monaghan and Wright, it was all right."

The 435-foot cantilevered tower intended to accompany the four-story pizza headquarters is pure Birkerts. It will lean fifteen degrees to the east. Monaghan will pay for it because he knows the publicity value of the one and only.

The Midwestern township quickly named the proposed structure the "Leaning Tower of Pizza," but the architect is approaching the project seriously. He sees it as a symbolic sculpture, a landmark in the tradition of the Eiffel Tower, the original Leaning Tower of Pisa or the Empire State Building. It is his opportunity to play with the dynamic tensions of gravity in a rural field, free from urban restrictions.

"Vertical is neutral and I've been working with the vertical all my life," Birkerts said. "And this is only fifteen degrees off...."

Many see echoes of the Russian Constructivist Vladimir Tatlin's Monument to the Third International in 1920. Tatlin regarded his structure as a political sculpture that could break the norm.

Birkerts has similar feelings. He, too, is trying to return excitement to architecture through structure rather than with the party hats postmodern towers sometimes wear. His recommendations for materials and finishing, if followed, could make this a real piece of architecture, and not a stunt.

"Do you think I am schizophrenic?" Birkerts asked after leading a critic through St. Peter's Lutheran Church in Columbus, Indiana.

No, not schizophrenic, but perhaps at a turning point. This was the building, completed in 1988, where Birkerts resynthesized himself after a difficult several years spent tossing around on architecture's unsettled seas in the mid-1980s.

The architect explains that St. Peter's was part of an eclectic period that also included the Duke University Law School and the Monaghan work. If viewed collectively, the projects represent the closest Birkerts has ever come to postmodernism's form or image-borrowing habits.

He doesn't put that label on the work, however. "It was just coincidence that these projects came together. Either very unusual clients or conditions had to be satisfied," he says. "Maybe the experience made me more patient with the past."

Monaghan's insistence on the Wright theme for the Domino's headquarters hit Birkerts the hardest. "It was the first time I was forced to inhale someone else's breath. I am nobody's disciple. Aalto is the only one I've looked at closely," he says.

The church was Birkerts' solace after the Domino's project, a refuge to Aalto, Saarinen, and the German tradition, which was appropriate because the congregation was primarily German.

The round brick front crashes into the orthogonal concrete back. This may represent the collision of Birkerts' love of Alvar Aalto's gentle forms and the hard, rectilinear expression of Louis I. Kahn, Marcel Breuer and other modernists he admires. But the structure is topped with yet another element of the architect's past: a 115-foot copper spire that recalls the early history of the Lutheran faith in Europe. It looks remarkably similar to the spire on the church of Birkerts' boyhood, also named St. Peter's, in Riga, Latvia. Inside, the church is a different thing again: a plan composed of two not-quite-concentric circles. They uphold the architect's conviction that when people gather, they do so in intimate circles, but never perfect circles. The irregularity expresses his belief that design should follow the organic principles of life. Nothing grows straight up or straight down; the human body is asymmetrical.

The great volume is a dance of daylight invited inside in typically ingenious, Birkerts ways. Some observers believe it enters in too many ways. But perhaps this was appropriate; in the design of this building he was reconstituting himself, and he used every element in his daylighting repertoire. The light falls on blond wood furniture and other details that Birkerts designed for the interior.

Pragmatic forces contributed to the design. The congregation could not afford an all-brick building. This explains the abrupt change in materials that is slightly ameliorated by the banded brick insets in the concrete that visually join the header courses on the rounded brick section of the building.

Birkerts' first design involved a sloped, more complex copper roof that fit naturally on the building. The fan-shaped roof planes corresponded to the orthogonal sections of the exterior walls, and, as in all his best work, the diverse geometries of the parts interlocked. The client couldn't afford it. In its place is a smaller and less complex lid. It keeps the rain out, but is not as expressive as Birkerts' first plan would have been.

Birkerts has moved on to other things. The geometries are becoming more complex and the allusions deeper. The triangular addition to the Law Building at Ohio State University encloses the existing structures with a dynamism no one expected.

Layerings and segmented forms also define the office, retail and residential use center that is part of the Novoli project in Florence. The additional challenge of this project is to merge it successfully into the existing pattern of the city and with the designs of the many other architects working on the 70-acre site.

Plans are also underway for a tower in Turin, Italy, and a sports center in Venice.

But Birkerts is electrified by the potential opportunity to design a new national archives for Latvia in Riga. If realized, it would be the first structure built in recent times without the sponsorship of the Soviet Union. The structure would hold the country's greatest treasures – its literature and music,

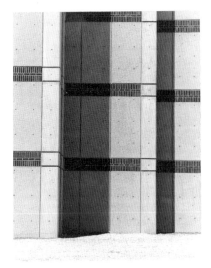

Detail of where brick and concrete meet at St. Peter's Lutheran Church in Columbus, Indiana.

compiled in part by the architect's own parents.

"The archives are what is left for us and what we will build upon for the future," he said. "That building will be the essence of what we are, and a monument to freedom."

He estimates that it must accommodate eight million volumes, which would make it one of the largest museum libraries in Europe. After an initial meeting to discuss the project, the architect is already thinking about how to bring the necessary library and construction technology to the country. Certain to come are material shortages. There is no wood and the native stone from Latvia's quarries is depleted.

There is brick, however. Birkerts will find a way.

"I am a realist. If I do it, it will be a labor of love."

The Method

As Birkerts matured, his approach to creativity changed to accommodate his increasing desire to design buildings that were individual responses to the client and meaningful to many people. The method he used to do this released information and experience stored in his subconscious. It is a region that transcends language, intellectual differences, and, most important, time. The designers of medieval cathedrals, he thinks, tapped into the secret, and Birkerts wanted to find the way, too.

In school he was taught the traditional mechanics of architecture. Parts of buildings were assembled in approved ways. This provided a solid base, but hardly took him where he wanted to go. Another method evolved during the work he did after hours in the Saarinen and Yamasaki offices.

"I worked with the 1-2-3 or hand-eye-brain sketching methodology," he explained in his book, Buildings, Projects and Thoughts, in 1985. "We all know the anguish of sitting in front of a sheet of white paper waiting for the force that will make us draw the first line. But in the 1-2-3 methodology, waiting is a mistake. Everything depends upon response, interaction and correction. The brain needs to be triggered by the hand as much as the hand by the brain. Draw two lines. The eye feeds that information to the brain. The brain tells you: 'Draw another line.' And the process starts."

The process involved continual sketching. "It was a step toward the conceptual, but I still had a long way to go...."

His process began to change around 1975, when he was approaching fifty, the age when many architects finally begin to trust themselves. Perhaps it takes that long to successfully synthesize a lifetime of experiences. Now he draws hardly at all, but visualizes the myriad of options every project suggests. This saves time and paper.

He considers the source of his inspiration to be his subconscious mind. It is as real to him as the forces in the universe scientists know are there, but cannot be perceived by the senses. Sometimes the physicist and the architect must accept something as real simply on the basis of its effect. This is often difficult for students to understand. It doesn't help when they ask Birkerts how he came upon a design concept and he honestly answers: "I don't know. I had nothing to do with it."

He is so saturated by images and meanings that he can no longer specify their origins. What he says sounds vaguely similar to Jungian psychology, many theories about free association and established approaches to learning and creativity. When he speaks about myths, he sounds as though he has read every book Joseph Campbell has written on the subject.

But Birkerts says he has read none. "And I didn't know I sounded Jungian until my daughter Andra told me I did when she gave me one of his books last Christmas."

So where do these ideas come from?

"They are just in the air," Birkerts answers. The explanation may be as good as any.

He does not consciously think of symbols or metaphors; they are usually identified by other people, after the building is designed.

Creative individuals in all disciplines have recognized and used the subconscious content of their minds. It is no secret that information from this source can cut through dissonances and chaff to deeper human responses. Most architects know about the subconscious influences in their work. Consequently, the concept is not unique to Birkerts.

It is unusual, however, to find an architect who maintains that his subconscious promptings are major components in his method. He gives himself over to them freely, fully relinquishing control.

But this happens only at the moment of conception. There is a precise and logical preamble to Birkerts' method: the extensive gathering of the facts from the client. This information mingles with elements from his past and his reaction to the present.

The answer comes after a period of relaxation or play: he bats a tennis ball around, goes to the theater or plants some flowers. Birkerts says he often works on a solution all night, in his dreams. Sometimes he seeks a catalyst from magazines. He will look through the pages for hours – not seeing the images necessarily, but allowing the subconscious to work.

"This incubation time starts the moment you are filled up to your ears with

Eliel Saarinen's Cranbrook School for Boys in Bloomfield Hills, Michigan (1925-1930). According to Saarinen's biographer, Albert Christ-Janer, "it was a combination of various influences working upon the architect, and from the sum of these he began his drawings."
Photo: Balthazar Korab.

information," he tells the students. "You can only hope that you have in your heritage the intelligence and the drive, the incentive to really come to the moment of creation. But you cannot force the solution out. The best way is to relax and do nothing."

Then, bang! It's there.

Call it spontaneous combustion, or divine intervention. Once Birkerts told architectural historian William Marlin it was the "sweep of the leap."

A loose, embryonic sketch is quickly drawn that usually contains all the elements the building needs. This drawing is checked and rechecked. His associate Anthony Gholz says that if the process works correctly, the concept is flexible enough to accommodate all the practical aspects of a project and even the unknown contingencies such as the four toilets no one thought the client needed originally.

And yet students are perplexed when Birkerts speaks of the subconscious synthesis of fact and feeling. It still seems made by magic. They are drawn instead by the allure of the measurable and repeatable, qualities not at the forefront of Birkerts' creative method. Their educational backgrounds have taught them to connect the parts of a building as prescribed, but the lessons have never included drawing the connections between psychology, physiology, history, architecture and, perhaps, metaphysics.

He gives students no formulas which allow them to draw by rote. Instead, he tells them to mine their own cultural and genetic backgrounds and to capture the vibrations of the current world. Birkerts urges them to remember the forms in their dreams and who said what. He tries to explain that this could have implications in their design, or reveal the real meaning behind a client's words. Hating green or "those pointy things at the corners" might not be the issue.

The directive to look within yourself is terrifying. It implies that the answer is within the individual, and either the student has the ability to tap into it, or he or she does not. This is often the first time the young architect is made aware of that indefinable "it quotient" that separates the great architects from the merely competent.

Birkerts continues to explain:

"The content of your brain is something that cannot be taken away by anybody. You have heard about so many people who have for many reasons abandoned their businesses or professions, or their countries. The only thing they could take with them, really, was what was in their heads – their knowledge and their heritage. Those things were their assets.

"The brain is the carrier of the genetic heritage. And it is supplemented continually by the cultural heritage and by the professional knowledge you acquire.

"I believe that I have existed since the beginning of life. Whether you believe in the Garden of Eden or the Big Bang, the continuity has never been interrupted.

"Whatever enters your brain through your ears or through your eyes is there forever.... And you know quite well that it can be retrieved. It is done in a conscious way that we call thinking. You can think in public, but if you want to make contact with the subconscious, you have to withdraw.

The four nodes at the center of Birkerts' conceptual sketch of the Ferguson house (1980) represent the inner functions. Also contained in the drawing is the idea that interior and exterior walls do not touch.

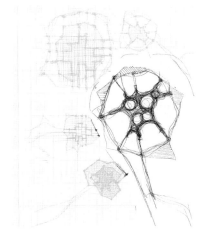

"This process is very slow. The information is deeply stored and can be recalled by hypnosis, but you can do it yourself if you can just get at it. In it is the inheritance from your father and his father before him. You don't have their knowledge, but you have their methodology. If he was a hard-working plumber, you have it in you to finish the job, but you don't know what he knew about soldering the pipes together...."

Most students have never heard of such things before. Birkerts seems like a Druid at Stonehenge who catches a lightning bolt and transforms it into the Corning Museum of Glass.

Birkerts found the clue to the Kalamazoo, Michigan, "Villa Ginny" house in an airplane over the Colorado Rockies. When the IBM Corporate Computer Center in Sterling Forest, New York, was designed in 1970, people's fear of computers was in the air. He included the red line that separated the human space from the computers as a reminder to those who worked there never to forget who was in control. The architect saw the film, "2001: A Space Odyssey," after the building was designed. In the story the line between artificial and human intelligence becomes blurred and havoc rocks the universe. After seeing the film, he knew he had tapped into the *Zeitgeist*.

There was something about Rome that unclogged the last remnants of gridlocked modernism in him while he was Architect-in-Residence at the Academy. The concept for the Corning Museum of Glass was born there. Perhaps it was the history that came in the softest waves from the stone. He can't explain exactly; his deepest metaphors and symbols "just happen," he says.

Eliel Saarinen's Cranbrook Academy of Art is another powerful subconscious source for Birkerts. As it is on the road between his home and office, its sloping roofs and textures are daily companions. Over the past thirty years, he has walked every inch of the grounds, absorbing the subtle asymmetries, the eclecticism and the ethnic references that gently stimulate Birkerts into remembering who he is and where he comes from.

When he drives past, his conscious mind may be on the presentation scheduled in the next hour, but the Cranbrook roofscape seen from the corner of his eye at forty miles an hour triggers many memories. Scandinavian light, Riga streets, the stone in Jean Sibelius's house in Finland, the farm buildings Hugo Häring designed near Lübeck and many other things dear to Birkerts come back strongly. One can be certain that similar elements will be incorporated in the drawings of the new building the architect presents after he parks the car in Birmingham, Michigan. The seconds of Cranbrook reaffirm their right to be on the paper.

This appreciation for Cranbrook's architecture came later in Birkerts' life. When he came to the United States, he thought the mid-1920s design was surprisingly antiquated, and couldn't believe it was of roughly the same vintage as Stuttgart's Weissenhofsiedlung.

As Birkerts further explains his design philosophy to students, one cannot avoid being struck with more similarities to Saarinen the elder, and lamenting that Birkerts did not meet him before he died. Eliel's book, *The Search for Form in Art and Architecture*, first published in 1948, concerns the roles instinct, the subconscious and intuition play in creativity.

Saarinen also urged his students to examine the way a tree grows and to marvel in that two are never alike. His lessons in design also involved flights into biology, psychology and other life sciences.

Saarinen makes a strong case for the acceptance of intangibles such as imagination and intuition. Both, he believed, were the connectors to primary facts and truths. "This is fully plain, and there is nothing more to say. For, whoever tries to elaborate on the matter soon becomes involved [in] a network of arbitrary assumptions," Saarinen wrote. "Thus someone has said: 'It is easy to know God, as long as one does not vex oneself to define Him.'"

Jean Sibelius's house near Helsinki, Finland, designed by Lars Sonck.

Birkerts considers intuition a legitimate tool of architectural synthesis: "It allows us to make the leap which we cannot rationally determine at that point in the design process. Later we come back and fill in the gap with research and thinking from the conscious mind, which is generally too clumsy to make the leap."

He laments that children today do not have the practice in visualization they once had. "Reading a fairy tale to a child is a wonderful tool for visualization. He or she in the mind's eye will see the image. And the problem with our young people now is that they have grown up under the television – the Saturday image of the cartoons running while the parents are sleeping late. But unless the child had a good story the night before, the visual imagination in the young mind will not develop."

Birkerts believes architecture students must know about current developments in art, music, literature and every other facet of contemporary life. "It is mandatory to be plugged into today," he said in a lecture at the University of Michigan. "If you look back into history and shortchange today, which the postmodernists did, what came out was a contorted, concocted architecture that did not advance our culture or our lives."

Birkerts is a proponent of organic architecture. The definition of organic has perplexed architects and writers for most of this century. Sigfried Giedion believed it was "anchored so deeply in the irrational unconscious" that even Frank Lloyd Wright could never precisely define it. Louis Sullivan came the closest, Giedion believes, when he wrote in *Kindergarten Chats* that the organic was the "ten-fingered grasp of reality."

The statement is related to Birkerts' conception. "The building grows from the seed into the form of the building and is responsive to the forces that are around it," he says. "The design responds to interior and exterior considerations, the *Zeitgeist* and the personality of the client.

"The building grows like a plant, but that doesn't mean it will look like one. When I say my work is organic, I am referring to my process, not my forms, necessarily."

Birkerts has never designed a building that looks like a seashell or a snowflake. His ornamentation has never consisted of abstractions of plant forms, and yet his work is organic at its heart. This fact makes his work with Tom Monaghan all the more interesting because Birkerts successfully stretched his client's understanding of the term.

He explained organic architecture this way in a lecture at the University of Michigan, Ann Arbor:

"Architecture is born. It is not constructed of pieces, but born out of the need that generates the form. Bruno Zevi wrote in his first book, *Towards an Organic Architecture*, that the organic is the search for the design of a particular building, for a particular case. The inorganic is the search for the universal, and that is the problem. The International Style is universal – and that's why we hear so much about the characterless boxes.

"Organic architecture seeks dynamic forms. They are generated, they move, they excel. But organic architecture is really anti-composition because it grows out of a need that tells you about the proportions, the rhythms, symmetry. You are not called upon to compose.

"Inorganic architecture is based on composition, and the worst of it is axial composition. There are very few buildings in the world that have to be symmetrical. But we like boxes that have windows here, windows there, and one in the middle. And a little pediment over the door and two columns.

"Organic architecture is like listening to a piece of music. You can never take in the entire piece at once. You have to listen to it from beginning to end several times. And if the orchestra played all the notes in the symphony at the same time, it would just be noise. It would break your eardrums. You must listen to it one note at a time.

"It is the same with organic architecture. The right side is not like the left side. The front doesn't look like the back. You have to see it all, just like you have to listen to that piece of music.

"Organic architecture has the opportunity to be expressive. It is architecture that needs to say something. Buildings have a duty in our society to say something whether they are churches, theaters, museums, or libraries. They are the buildings of the spirit."

It is interesting that Birkerts equates the ability to relax and mental repose with the new spark of creativity that came in 1975. "The commissions were coming, my work was getting published and my self-confidence had increased greatly. Self-confidence and creativity are not unrelated," he says.

Curiously, as if life and architecture actually are related, his work began to grow more relaxed, too. It took on more natural, segmented forms and deeper meanings. The Corning Museum of Glass, the Iowa College of Law and the yet-unbuilt addition to the Cathedral of the Most Blessed Sacrament in Detroit are examples of this change.

His entry in the Minnesota History Center competition in 1984 clearly shows a tendency to draw upon the geological forms the structure is built upon. Plans for the underground addition to the library at the University of California, San Diego, reflect the rough-cut cliffs that lead down to the sea. The addition to the Oberlin Conservatory of Music Library responsively meets the existing building with walls that bend and move. It brings to mind the way indigenous builders of ancient cities added something new to their streets.

Birkerts can identify one of the sources of these images. They come from his favorite place in the world – his restored home in Civita di Bagnoregio, a 2,300-year-old Italian hill town built on Etruscan wine cellars two hours north of Rome.

For the last twenty years, the architect and his family have spent summer holidays and other special times at this 500-foot-high rock outcropping in a chestnut forest. "It is built on the stone and is of the stone. It is completely

The Civita house in an early stage of reconstruction in 1969.

above:
Civita di Bagnoregio, showing Birkerts' house just above the cliff at the left side of the picture.

homogeneous," he says, fully cognizant of the rarity.

It is his place of deepest repose. Since the relaxed mind is the condition that invites creativity, it is natural, then, that Civita's shapes and equally distinct qualities of spirit should influence his architecture.

Civita seen in plan is a cluster of irregularly shaped and spaced buildings that conform to the layerings of the mountain. They were built by many different hands over many generations according to their needs and inclinations. Birkerts delights in the polygonal configurations that make any academic definition of organic absurd. Nothing is square, symmetrical or ordered in any coldly theoretical way. It just grew.

It grew from the tufa, a soft and porous limestone, that was cut out of the cliff. Birkerts inhales these things. He senses the history that emanates from deep in the stones. This is real history, not the kind made in extrusion molds. He believes all architects need to live with these things at some time in their lives.

The walls of his own house and terrace move in and out with the edge of the cliff, and daylight comes in from many angles. Traces of these forms can easily be picked out in his plans for the Novoli mixed-use project in Florence, and in many other designs over the last ten years. Even the segmented structure of the long foot bridge that flies over a great gulf in the terrain and provides the only access to Civita, looks vaguely familiar after one spends time looking at his work in plan.

When he is not there, he is reminded of Civita by the photographs on the dining room wall of his Bloomfield Hills, Michigan, home. They were taken by Balthazar Korab, who owns two unrestored houses in Civita. The peppery Korab and Birkerts have been friends for more than thirty years, ever since they worked in Saarinen's office. Both grow dreamy when they talk about the town above the chestnuts.

The early photographs of Birkerts' property at the edge of the cliff show a ruin. There is little differentiation between the stone hill and the building. Architect Astra Zarina, family friend and former colleague at Yamasaki's office, introduced Birkerts to Civita after she renovated a home for herself there. It was she who designed and supervised the reconstruction of the Birkerts property over a five-year period.

It was rebuilt stone by stone. The sinks and toilet came over the bridge by mule. It took ten men and two mules to bring in the high chest Sylvia and he found. He repainted the interior of the house himself. Because he wasn't certain that Tuscan village stores carried paint rollers, he packed them among his socks on several trips to Italy. The architect was enchanted that water-based paint was still called "tempera" in Italy.

Inside the house are white walls and chestnut beams, arched openings between rooms, irregularly shaped window openings and tile floors. He has many pictures of the sun coming through them and falling on simple furniture and flowers in vases.

The flowers come from the terrace garden. Ivy grows up the walls and is clipped back only at the edges of the windows. "See that red and white umbrella?" Birkerts asks, pointing to a speck in a photograph taken of Civita from a distance. "That is where you will find me. It is my reward for all the work, for all the grief, and for all the times architecture has taken me away from my family."

Gunnar and Sylvia have three children: Sven Peter, who was born in 1951; Andra Sylvia, born in 1954; and Erik Gunnar, born in 1967. The father thinks of the family as the fingers of a hand. "There are five of us and together we are strong. Remember, we are the immigrants and the children the first born in America. We stick together."

Sylvia remembers the names and dates and does not appear to have suffered unduly from a lifetime with a man who eats, sleeps and breathes architecture.

"The Latvian people persevere," she said in a conversation intended to explain her husband. "If he was a pushover, I wouldn't be with him."

There is a quality about Civita that makes Birkerts examine how fate worked upon his family. The architect is curious about how his interests and those of his parents were passed on to his own children despite the gaps in time and geography.

Sven Peter is a literary critic based in Boston and a teacher at Harvard University. Sections in his first two books examine the creative process as it applies to literature. His specialty is contemporary European writers.

Daughter Andra is a graphic designer in Boston. Her abstract and energetic paintings dominate many rooms in the Birkerts Michigan home. Erik Gunnar, the youngest, whose childhood was photographically recorded amid the tufa of Civita, is now studying international law.

Thinking about these things is possible in Civita because of the history and the extraordinary kindness of the site and the people. He feels at home with the simplicity and the elegance such simplicity brings. It is consistent with his Latvian heritage.

The atmosphere helps to reinforce his own lyricism. Although he tells his students to be intimately connected to the *Zeitgeist*, he also believes creative people must separate themselves from its negative aspects from time to time. "There is dishonesty and corruption, and generally the things you saw happening in the war are happening right now in our own peacetime," he says.

Birkerts renews himself in Civita and everywhere else he goes. It's just easier to do in Italy, a country populated by people with a tendency to revere and indulge architects.

"I have to stay lyrical," he says. It is the only way he can impart to his architecture the compassion and inspiration he wants people to feel in it.

"I really believe that what I want to do is progress and invent because I know there is a different answer for the same problem a year from now," he says.

"In our lifetimes we educate ourselves, we adapt new technologies, we create and we progress. Our development is based on organic growth, as are our best buildings. It is an evolution, a progression, and that is what I believe I am doing. I am growing and evolving in the time span in which I am destined to live and be creative."

His architecture and the influences it represents are like the currents in that great Baltic Sea of his childhood. They merged with the American tides, broke apart into eddies and reformed again and again. But their nature was always unmistakably his, and his nature always theirs.

Selected Projects, 1957 – 1989

Note: The two dates assigned to most
entries are the date of design and the
date of completion.

Mequon House

Mequon, Wisconsin, 1957 (project)

This small residence on Lake Michigan was designed as an all-wood "living platform" that spans a ravine. A system of bridgelike trusses supports the house, but the bases on the floor of the ravine are small. The idea was to disturb the surroundings as little as possible while providing unbroken views of the lake and nearby bluffs. This was Birkerts' first Design Citation Award from *Progressive Architecture*.

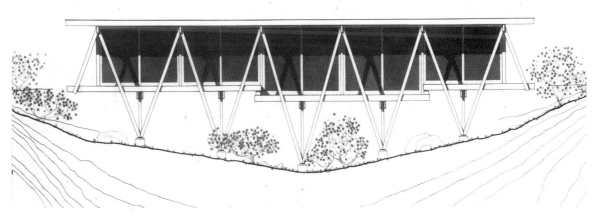

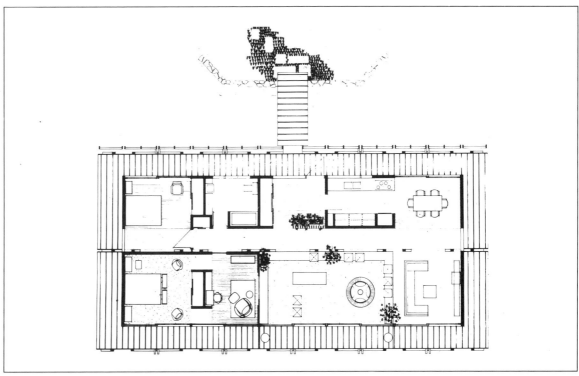

Cultural Center of Leopoldville

Leopoldville, Belgian Congo, 1958
(project)

The Belgian government sponsored
an international competition for a
cultural center master plan that
included government functions,
several museums, art galleries, office
space and places for public
gatherings. The architectural
determinant was a square planning
module separated by narrow
circulation-space modules located
under overhangs. These provide
design coherence while answering
the need for flexible expansion and
protection from the elements. The
plan was submitted with Astra Zarina
and Doug Hanner. It received third
prize.

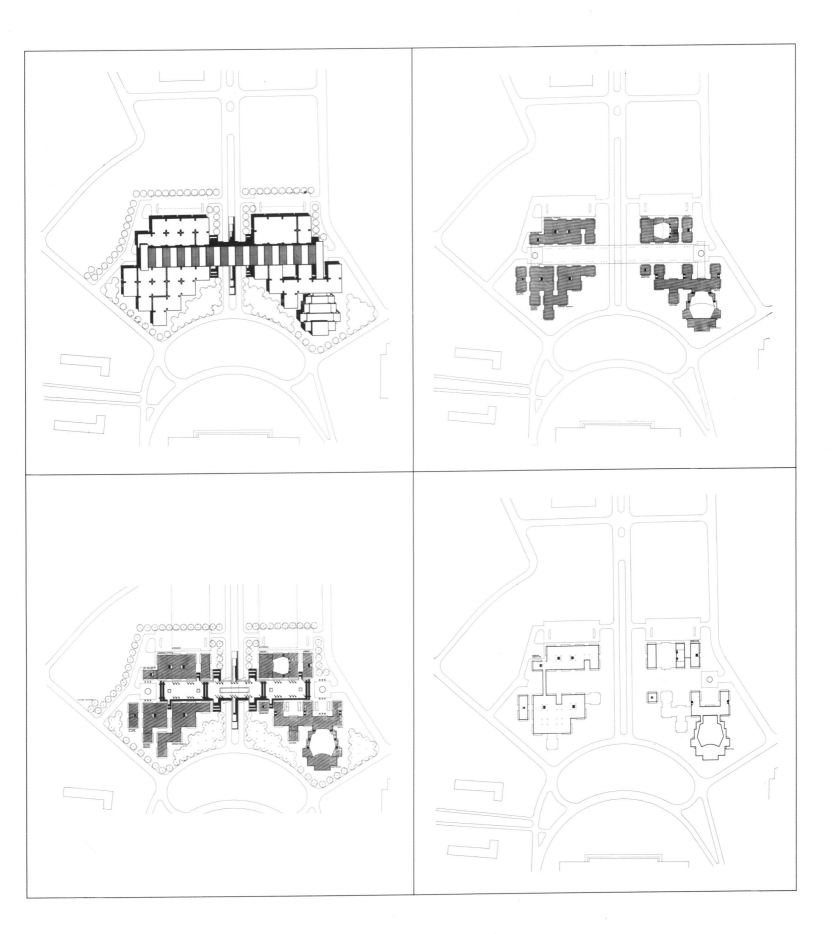

Technical University Competition
Ankara, Turkey, 1959 (project)

The complex, sited on a terraced plateau, closely responds to the topography. The open spaces formed by the buildings provide much-needed physical and psychological shelter from the sun and winds of the plains. Framed views of hills and of the city of Ankara ensure a connection to the outside. Piers and bearing walls form standard spatial and structural units that define the modular, expandable master plan. The project was submitted in collaboration with Astra Zarina, Jose Teran, and others.

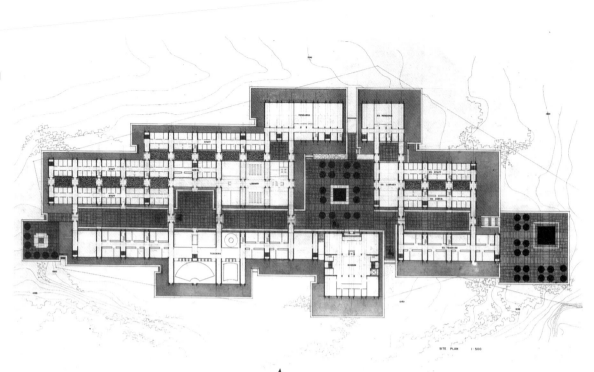

Schwartz Summer Residence

Northville, Michigan, 1960 (1962; destroyed 1986)

Placed in a 400-acre apple orchard, this house responded to the order of a tree-planting grid. The resulting Palladian symmetry was offset by an asymmetrical entrance. The image was one of concrete, but the structure was wood.

Haley Funeral Home

Southfield, Michigan, 1960 (1961)

This building is expressive of its function and projects the dignity and serenity of the event. Birkerts was opposed to making it look like an American country club. Instead, the imagery is timeless and related to steep-roofed Swedish and Finnish cemetery chapels, particularly Erik Gunnar Asplund's in Stockholm.

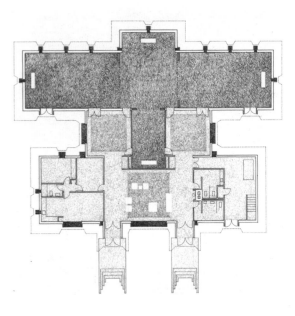

Albion Church

Albion, Michigan, 1960 (project)

The nave of this church is treated as a symbolic space that ascends toward the altar in a dynamic motion and rises toward ever-increasing intensity of light. "I regret that the church was never built," Birkerts writes. "It did, however, give me the opportunity to think new thoughts that would result in subsequent explorations of space and the use of daylight."

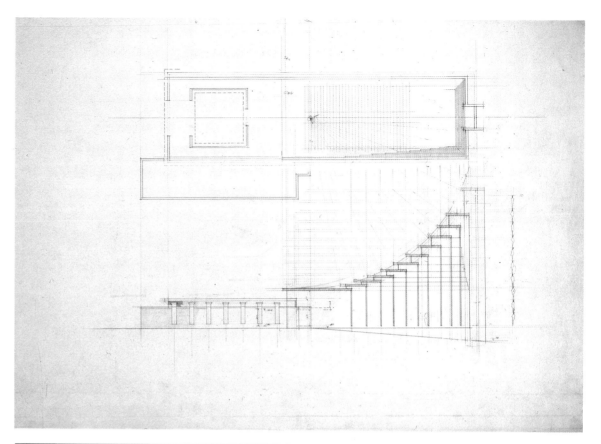

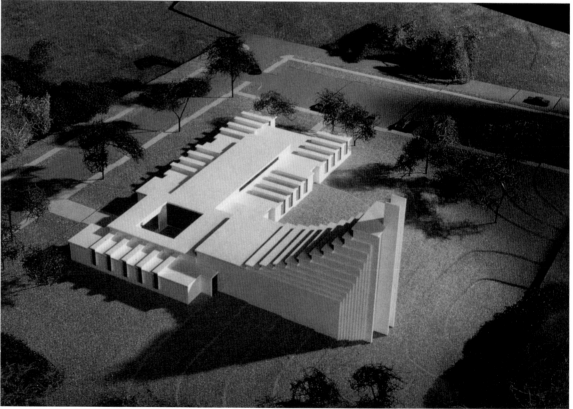

1300 Lafayette East Apartments
Detroit, Michigan, 1961 (1963)

In this reinforced concrete building, at the time of its construction the highest in Detroit, form is uninhibited by structure. The variable column spacing is a reflection of the apartment plans within. In the architect's words, "Structure must be subordinated to spatial needs, but it nevertheless can be expressive."

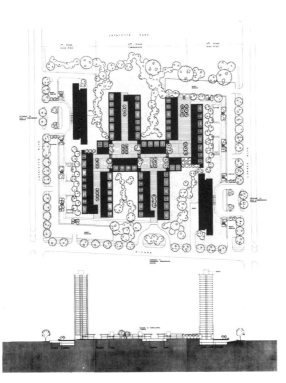

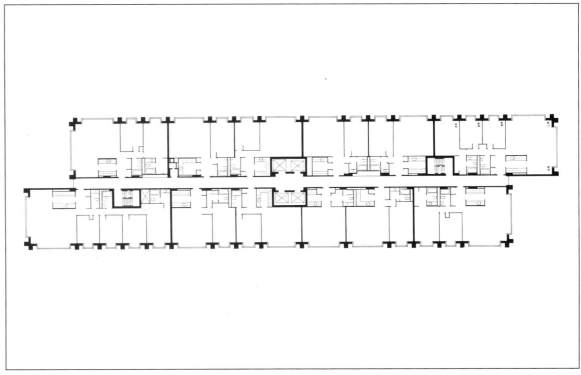

Marathon Oil Office Building

Detroit, Michigan, 1962 (1964)

This building, an early use of metal curtain wall, was designed to withstand the polluted atmosphere of a refinery site. Horizontal mechanical ducts are placed outside the building line. The projections create shade, convenient work surfaces for building cleaning and the structure's architectural definition.

Lillibridge Elementary School Addition
Detroit, Michigan, 1962 (1963)

The design of this building, located in a residential section of the inner city, breaks down its scale and responds to the vernacular structures around it. The interior plan is compact and without corridors. Classrooms are organized around an activity center. "The departure here was in the planning of spaces, in the conscientious use of daylight, and in our decision to use wood as the interface between the children and the abrasive masonry," the architect explains.

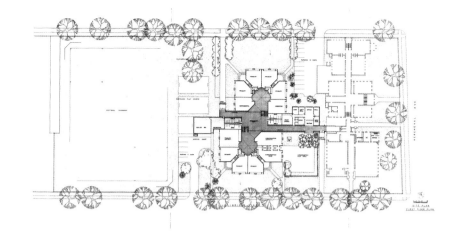

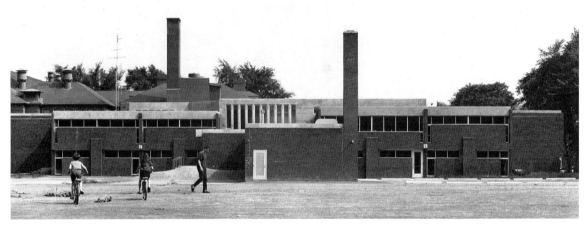

Peoples Federal Savings & Loan Bank, Branch Office
Royal Oak, Michigan, 1962 (1963)

This small concrete building is symmetrical in plan but asymmetrical in its exterior wall development and structure. Vertical structure flanks the openings through the wall and the light-diffusing corners. The roof is separated from the walls by a layer of glass of varying depth.

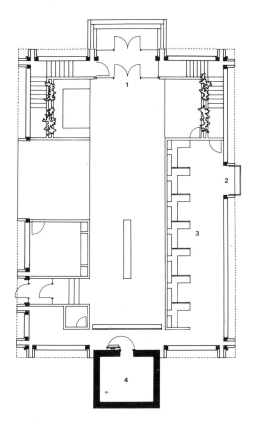

University Reformed Church

Ann Arbor, Michigan, 1963 (1964)

The basilicalike space of this church is formed by exposed concrete planes in the walls and ceiling beams. The symmetry of the space is relieved by asymmetrical altar development. Daylight is admitted between the upward-stepping sidewalls and is diffused and reflected into the interior. Concrete and wood are the materials. As with the Lillibridge School (1962), the architect chose to place wood where people and the structure touched.

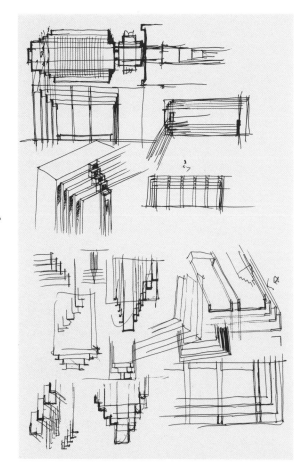

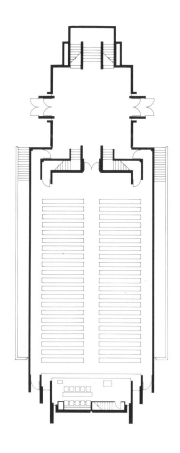

Bald Mountain Recreational Facility

Pontiac, Michigan, 1964 (1969)

The materials for this open-air swimming facility are poured concrete, timber and copper. The intent was to meld the structures organically into the landscape and to provide an aspect of permanence.

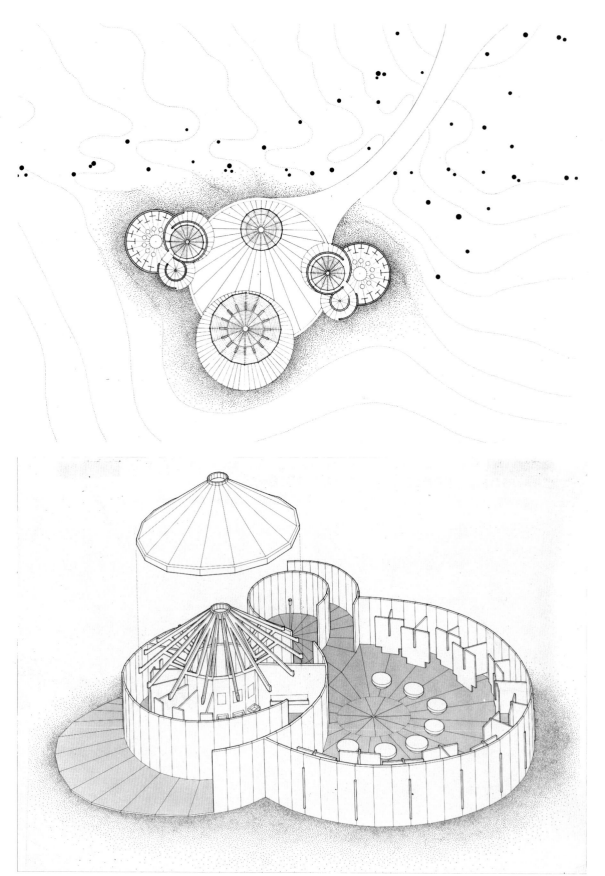

**Detroit Institute of Arts
South Wing**
Detroit, Michigan, 1964 (1964)

The addition to the museum's formidable Paul Cret building alludes to the base, shaft and cornice of a classical column. The design also challenges classical form by dissolving the corners in glass and by lifting the roof off the exterior walls.
The scale of Cret's structure is reflected in the new building's strong fascia and in subtle projections in the granite skin that correspond to the floor lines.

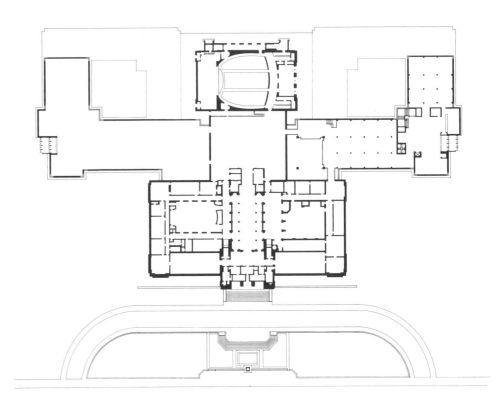

Fisher Administrative Center

University of Detroit, Detroit,
Michigan, 1964 (1966)

This building is treated as a symbolic
structure that expresses the spirit
and aspirations of the Jesuit order.
The design had to echo the
Mission-style buildings of the
campus, yet also represent the
forward-looking spirit of the university.
Dignity is suggested through the
structure and the use of color. The
roof, suspended over a sheet of
glass, is a contemporary device that
represents modernity.

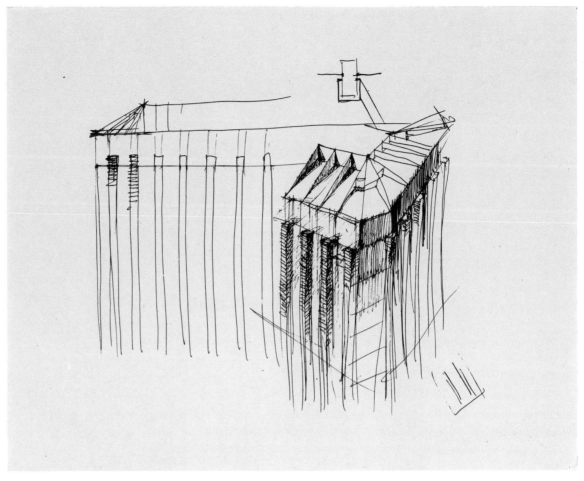

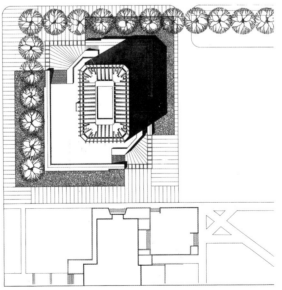

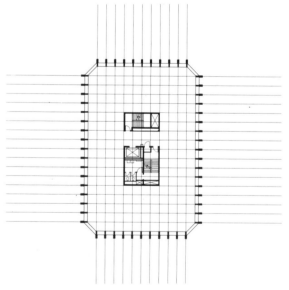

Travis Residence

Franklin, Michigan, 1964 (1965)

This suburban house for a family of four uses traditional wood construction with brick and metal exterior materials. Varied room sizes and heights are expressed in the articulated exterior form. Roof projections are punctured as necessary to admit daylight.

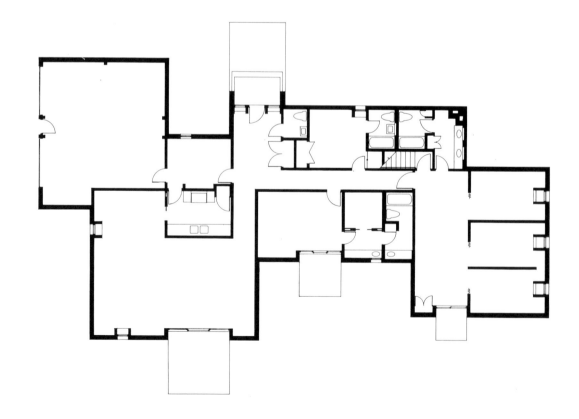

Freeman Residence
Grand Rapids, Michigan, 1965 (1966)

In this house, the superimposition of an orthogonal over a radial planning grid generates unconventional two- and three-dimensional spaces and structure while allowing conventional roof framing. The center of the radiating grid is placed eccentrically in the atrium space, the hub of the house. Wall and ceiling planes reflect and diffuse light throughout the interior.

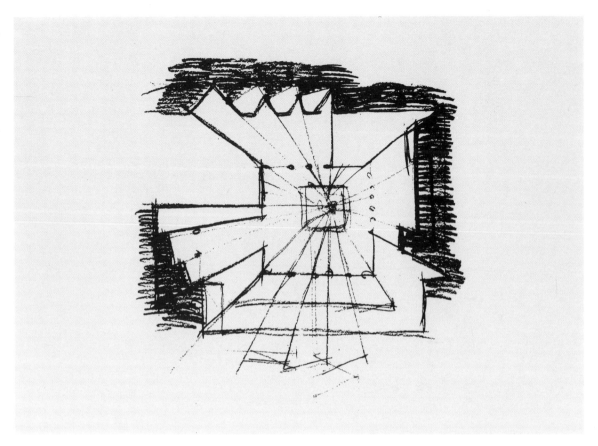

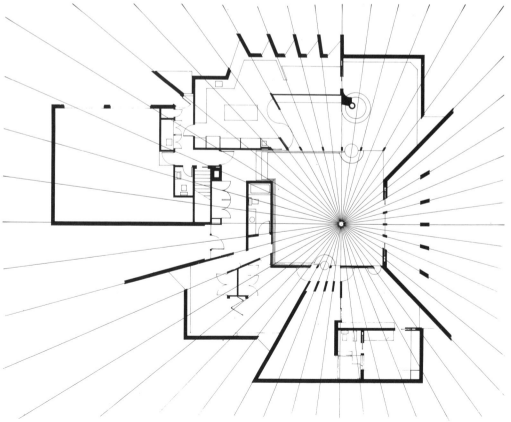

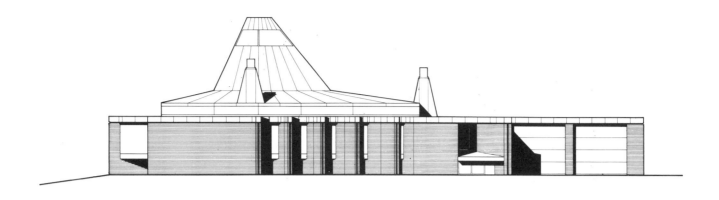

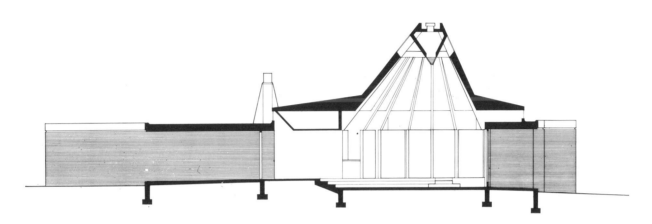

Lincoln Elementary School
Columbus, Indiana, 1965 (1967)

This understated public building is the simplest architectural form: a square within a circle. Because the school was to be an important part of the community, the building returns the urban block to the use of the neighborhood around it. The square is depressed a half-level below ground and is further screened by a ring of trees. The concrete and brick structure is highly energy efficient because of the minimal perimeter and innovative fenestration.

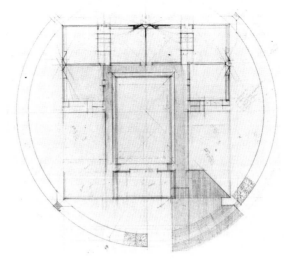

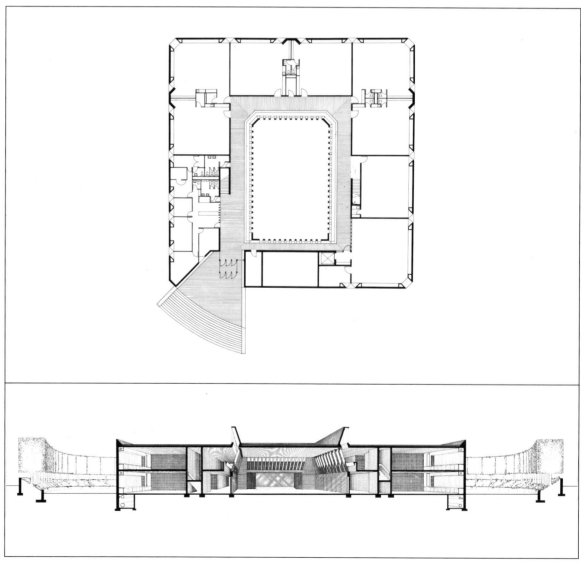

Livonia Public Library

Livonia, Michigan, 1965 (1967)

This small civic building on a large piece of land had to establish its presence on a heavily traveled street. Roof geometries and the triangular, asymmetrical plan do the announcing. Articulated library spaces receive north light from the top and gain heat from the south. The strategically placed main desk controls all entrances and reading spaces.

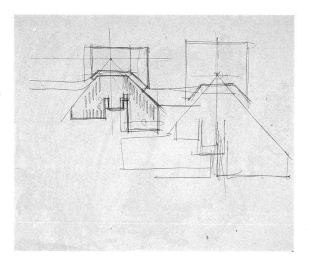

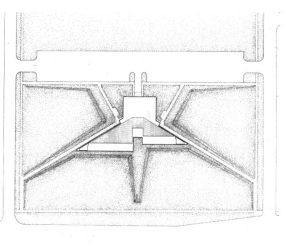

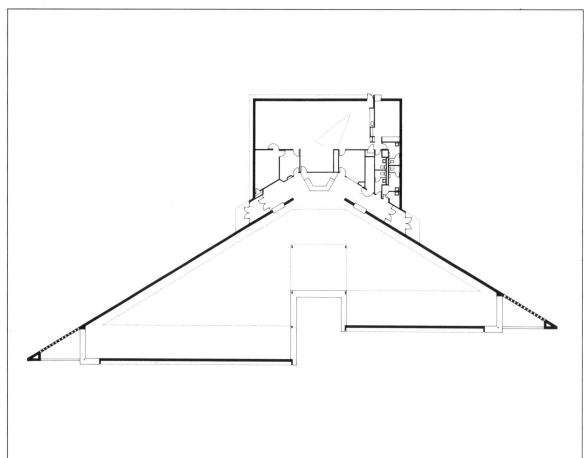

**Tougaloo College Campus
Master Plan**
Tougaloo, Mississippi, 1965 (project)

The layered concept of this master
plan system allows for functional,
structural and mechanical growth.
Interior and exterior spaces employ
similar architectural vocabulary. The
building program involved only the
two dormitory units and the library.

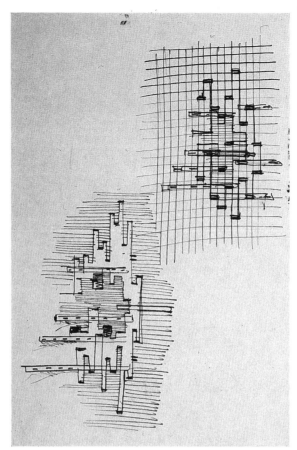

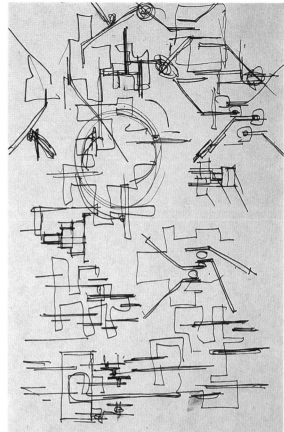

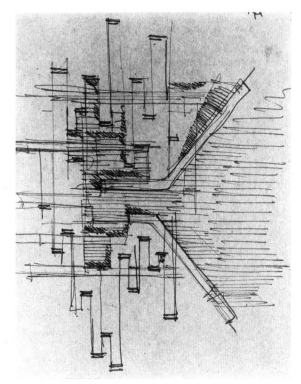

Massey Ferguson North American Operations Offices

Des Moines, Iowa, 1966 (project)

This project for a farm machinery manufacturer proposed wrapping an existing office building in an office space addition and a large parts assembly plant. The existing land form was to be shifted into a berm that rose toward the building and concealed the parking underneath the building. The proposed skin system was double glass with air-conditioned and ventilated space in between.

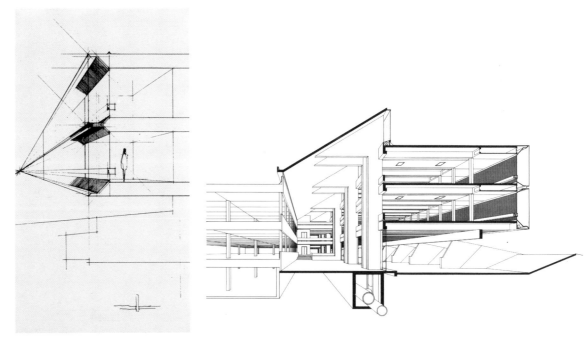

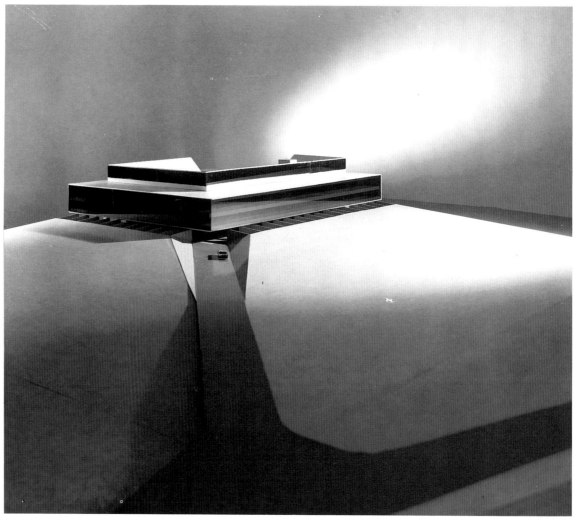

Glen Oaks Community College
Centreville, Michigan, 1966 (1971)

The strong spinal concept in this master plan carries the provision for linear expansion in either direction from a point in the center. Structural and mechanical systems permit extension in all four directions. Exterior walls are precast panels that can be moved for flexibility.

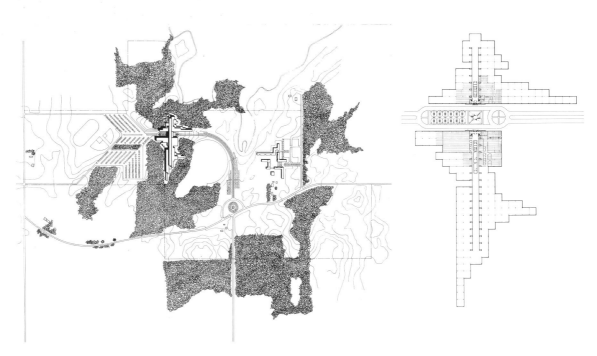

Tougaloo College Dormitories and Library
Tougaloo, Mississippi, 1966 (1972)

The residential "street" of this layered master plan contains student dormitories (p. 65) and faculty housing. The house concept is based on a common living space with dormitory rooms clustered around it. Faculty housing occurs intermittently throughout the plan. The library (pp. 62-64) is a series of staggered lofts. The multistoried central spaces rise diagonally to create an upward movement that spatially and visually unifies all the floors. The structural system is a combination of precast and poured-in-place concrete. The square grid provides a flexible, expandable matrix for the library and accommodates most of the architectural conditions that might need to be solved in the matrix.

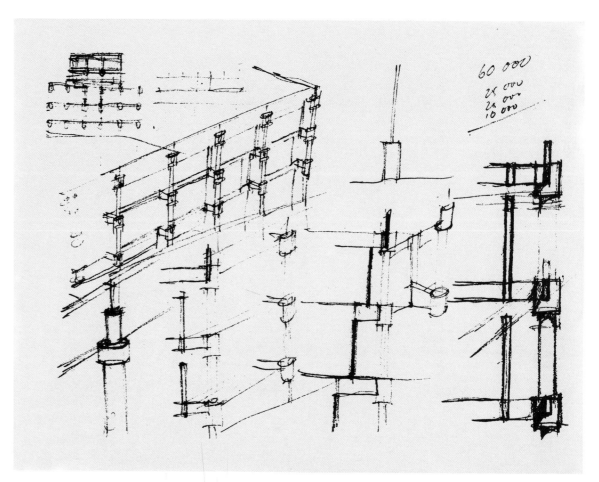

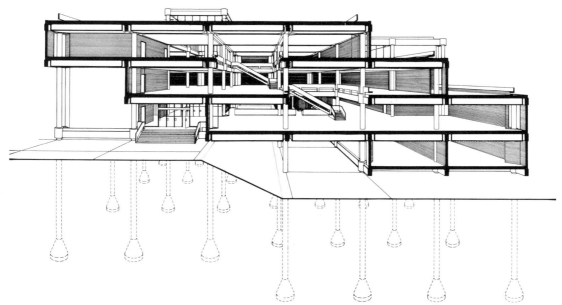

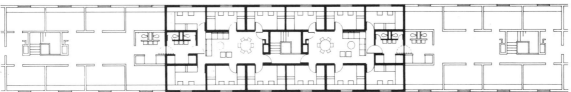

SECOND FLOOR

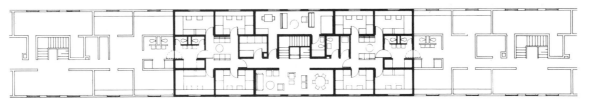

FIRST FLOOR

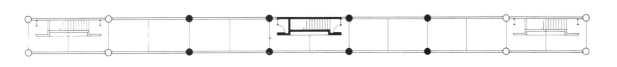

BRIDGE

0 5 10
| | |

Church of St. Bede
Southfield, Michigan, 1966 (1969)

The rising roof planes of this church capture light, while the asymmetrical plan and roof enclosure bring dynamic qualities into the space. The design relates to the sweeping changes made in the Roman Catholic liturgy in the 1960s.

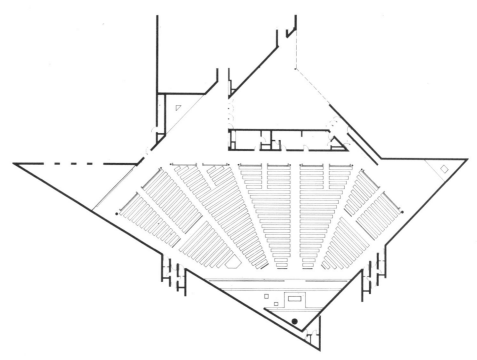

Vocational Technical Institute Campus Master Plan
Carbondale, Illinois, 1967 (project)

This flexible planning concept treats buildings as kinetic units, as though they were movable on a set of tracks. The image is of ships at dockside, which are easy to move around as need demands.

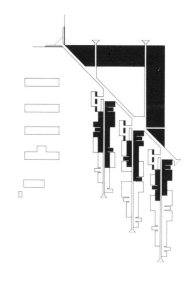

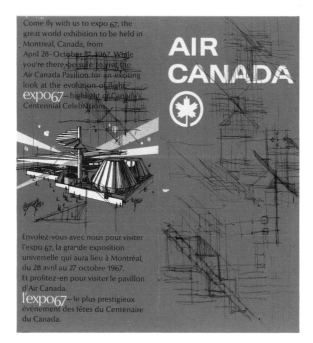

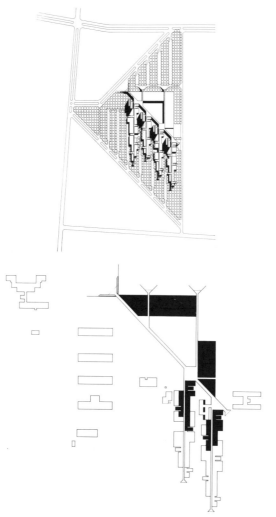

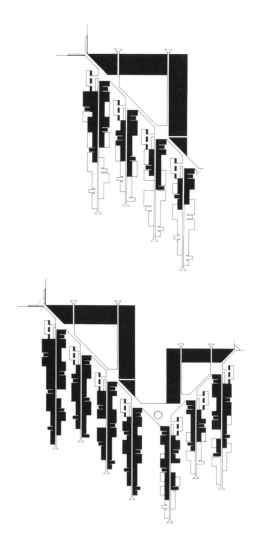

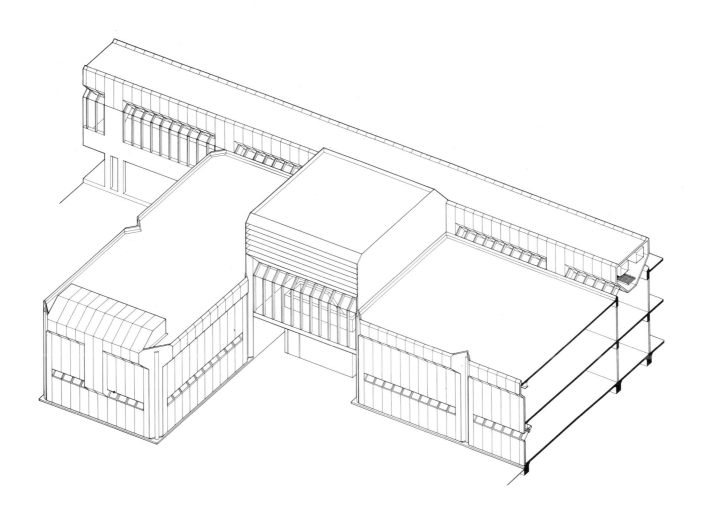

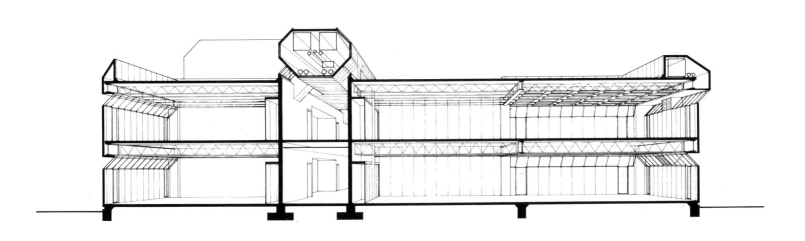

Ford Pavilion of Hemisfair '68
San Antonio, Texas, 1967 (1968)

"Here was my chance to design a structure with a short life-span – with no pressure of posterity!" Birkerts has written. The temporary exhibition building employed a lattice steel structural system with corrugated metal siding and a vinyl fabric membrane on laminated wood beams. It held a movie theater, an outdoor area for display, and an administration area.

Amsterdam City Hall Competition
Amsterdam, Netherlands, 1968
(project)

Even though the program for the Amsterdam City Hall suggested a large building mass, every effort was made to keep this design in scale with the surrounding buildings. The site was an island with canals and bridges nearby. The city government wanted to maintain an open door policy, and Birkerts thought the architecture should, too. Thus this design is open and transparent.

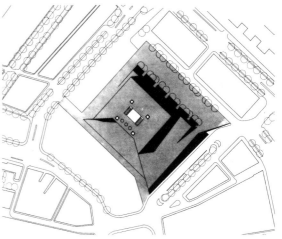

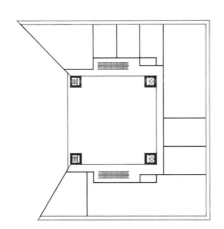

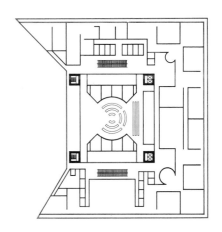

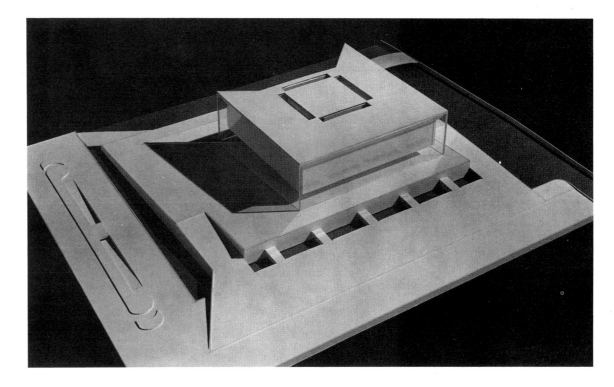

Federal Reserve Bank of Minneapolis

Minneapolis, Minnesota, 1968 (1973)

The design was conceived as two distinct buildings in direct response to two dissimilar demands in the program. The first structure contains high security functions below the plaza, which slopes upward 22 feet from grade. The second contains an office tower that bridges 330 feet across the top of the plaza, from street to street. The catenary suspension allows for future expansion vertically. The bank is an urban sculpture that responds to the vast scale of the Northern Plains. Some see it as a gateway, and feel the honesty of its structure and use of materials expresses a regional character trait.

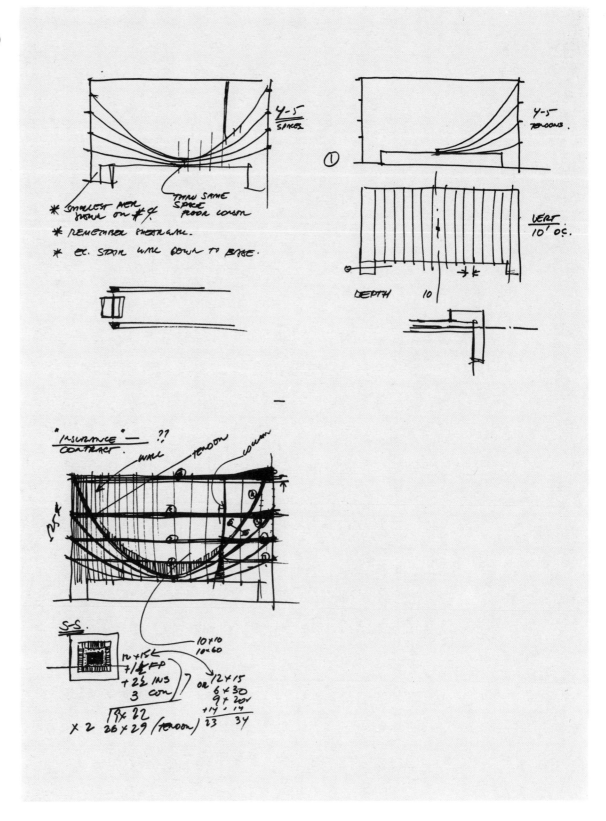

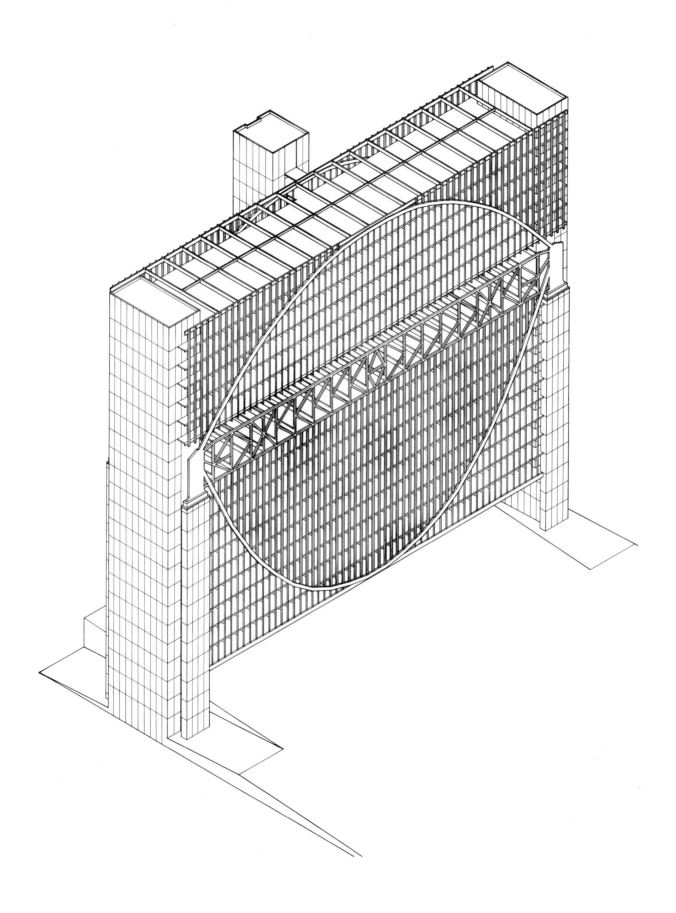

Corning Public Library
(first proposal)
Corning, New York, 1969 (project)

The city of Corning is divided by the Chemung River, but the library had tc belong to the entire city, not one side or another. This first proposal made the building a bridge that spanned the river. The scale was minimized by faceting the outer edges to conform with the terrain. The concept was abandoned because city buildings had to be built on city land rather than on a publicly owned riverbed.

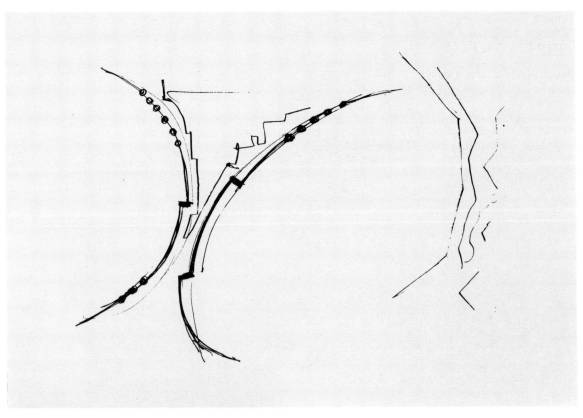

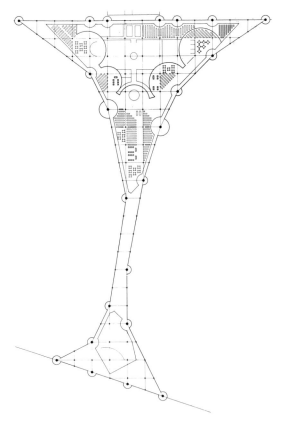

Corning Public Library
(final proposal)
Corning, New York, 1969 (project)

This proposal contains a strong
metaphor: the circle encompasses
the extent of present human
knowledge, and the prismatic glass
breakthroughs suggest the quest for
knowledge beyond the present limits.
The two semicircular formations have
practical functions: one is formal
space containing stack areas and
work spaces; the other holds open
stacks, reading areas for children
and adults, and reference facilities.

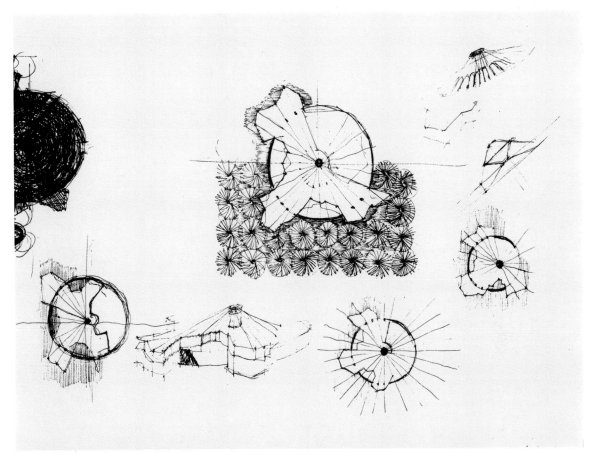

Dance Instructional Facility
State University of New York,
Purchase, New York, 1971 (1976)

The underlying metaphor of this
design is a garden surrounded by a
thick wall. The spaces inside the wall
contain studios that become like
pavilions. The garden wall slopes
toward the inside, gathering daylight
and reflecting it into the corridors and
studios. The attenuated corridors
were dictated by the narrow site, and
they in turn determined the character
of the building.

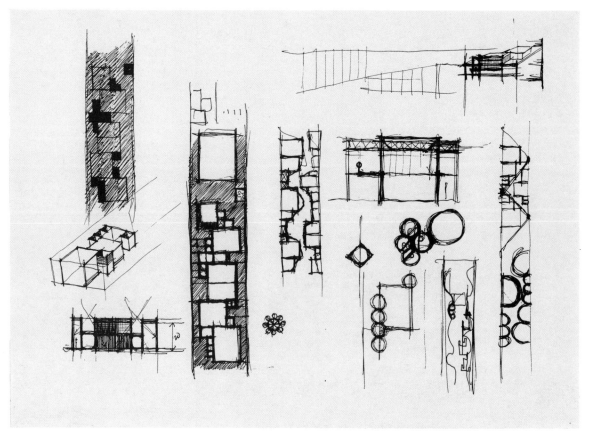

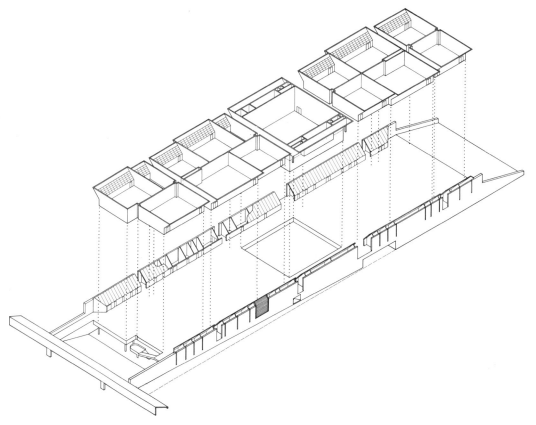

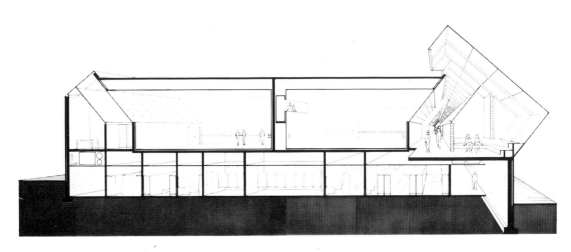

IBM Corporate Computer Center
Sterling Forest, New York, 1970 (1972)

The concept for the IBM Corporate Computer Center contrasts the building technology sharply with the natural setting. The mirrored surface symbolically and literally reflects the present. The glass and polished metal curtain wall encloses the simplest form – the cube. The form and materials were determined by the client's budget and the technical specifications for the interior.

Outdoor Chapel, Latvian Center, Garezers

Three Rivers, Michigan, 1972 (1972)

Standard square oak timbers were used in this construction. The rustic assemblage expresses the sometimes austere character of Nordic Lutheran congregations. Birkerts considered the project a wonderful opportunity to design symbolic, functional sculpture that had its basis in nature and people, not high technology.

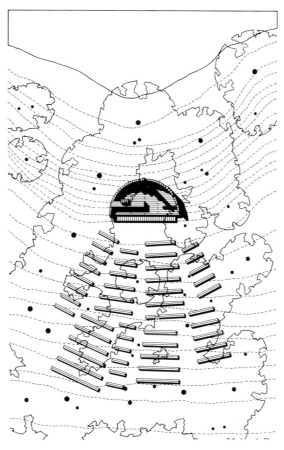

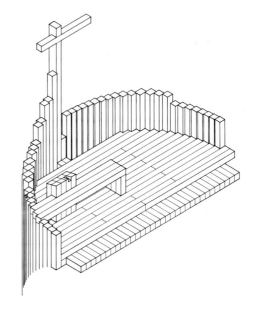

Contemporary Arts Museum
Houston, Texas, 1970 (1972)

This structure presents itself as a scaleless minimal sculpture caught between residential development on one side and the Museum of Fine Arts by Mies van der Rohe on the other. Its angled stainless steel walls reflect and deflect traffic. The museum director wanted an obstacle-free space that would accommodate any experiment in modern art; thus, the interior is an uninterrupted workshop-like area spanned by a space frame structure.

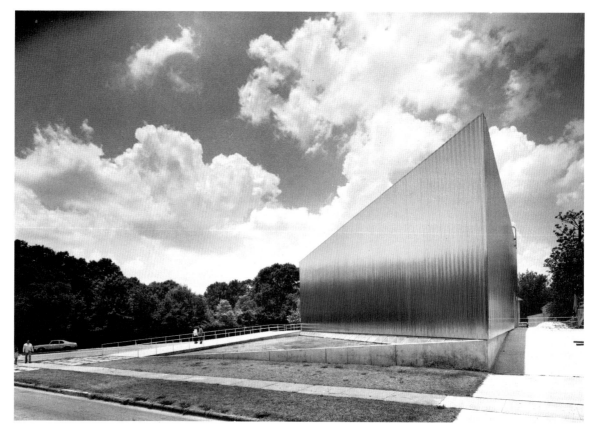

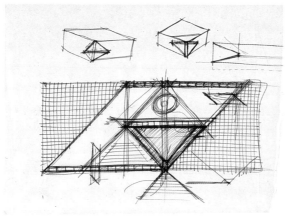

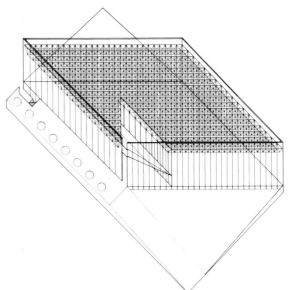

Municipal Fire Station

Corning, New York, 1973 (1974)

This building acts as a pointer in the landscape: when seen from the rim of the valley, one side points to downtown Corning and another to the Corning Glass Center. At the same time, the triangular form fulfills internal practical and programmatic needs. The station's iconography is clear: the fittings, gaskets, color, and other finishes associated with fire trucks are used in the building.

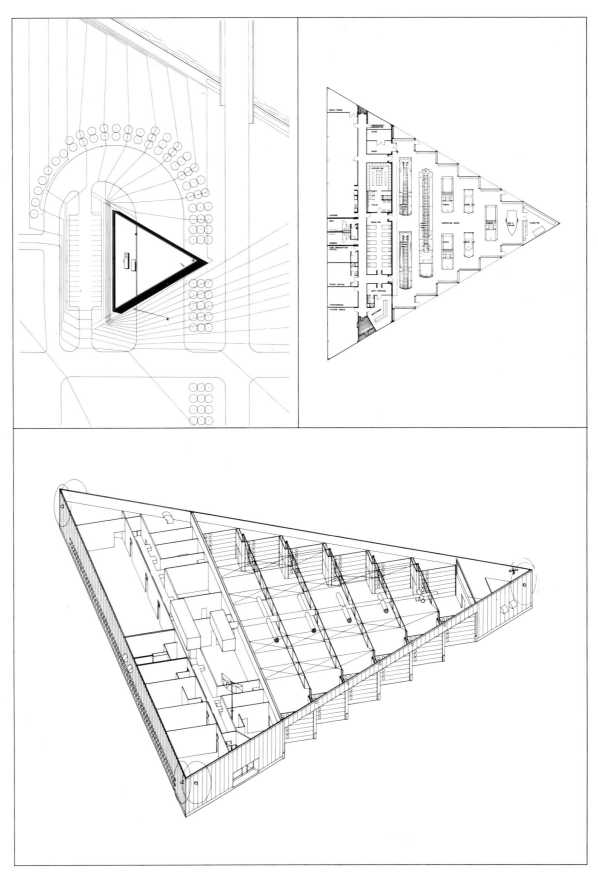

Calvary Baptist Church
Detroit, Michigan, 1974 (1977)

This building is a strong, simple, large-scale sculpture sited on a green next to a wooded cemetery. The geometry of the structure and its bright orange ribbed metal exterior are intended to be as lively as the congregation. Inside, the people face an immense mirrored and faceted wall surface. Birkerts' motivation was to bring people together visually and spiritually.

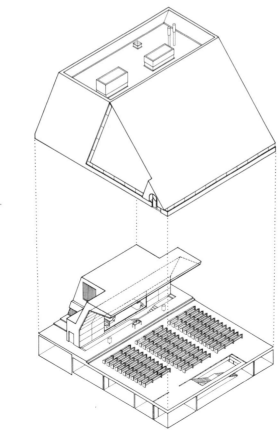

University of Michigan Law School Addition

Ann Arbor, Michigan, 1974 (1981)

A three-story underground building was the solution to minimize change to an existing faux-Gothic library. The L-shaped plan wraps the existing library and extends to the adjacent streets. A V-shaped trough brings light underground. The limestone side forms a base for the existing library and reflects light deep into the interior from the glazed side. Supporting mullions are clad in mirrors, which reflect daylight and fragmented images of the older library.

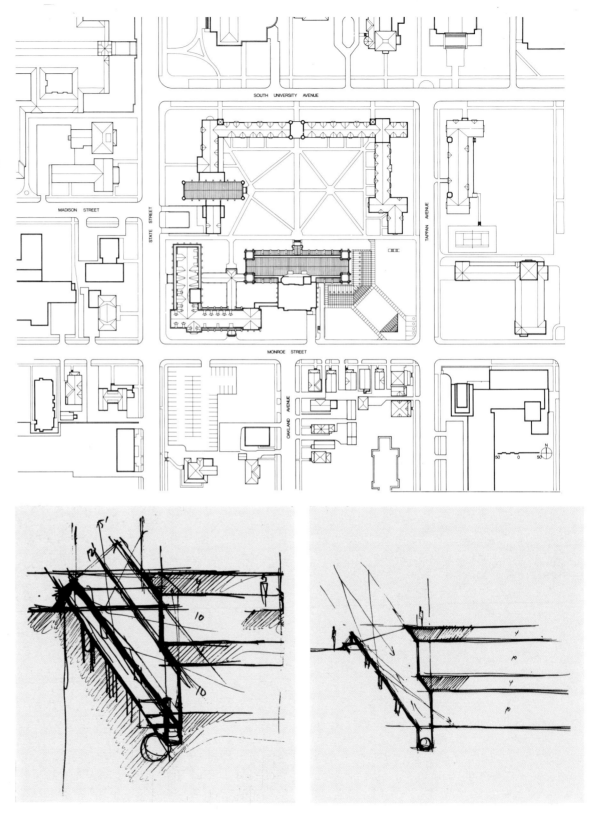

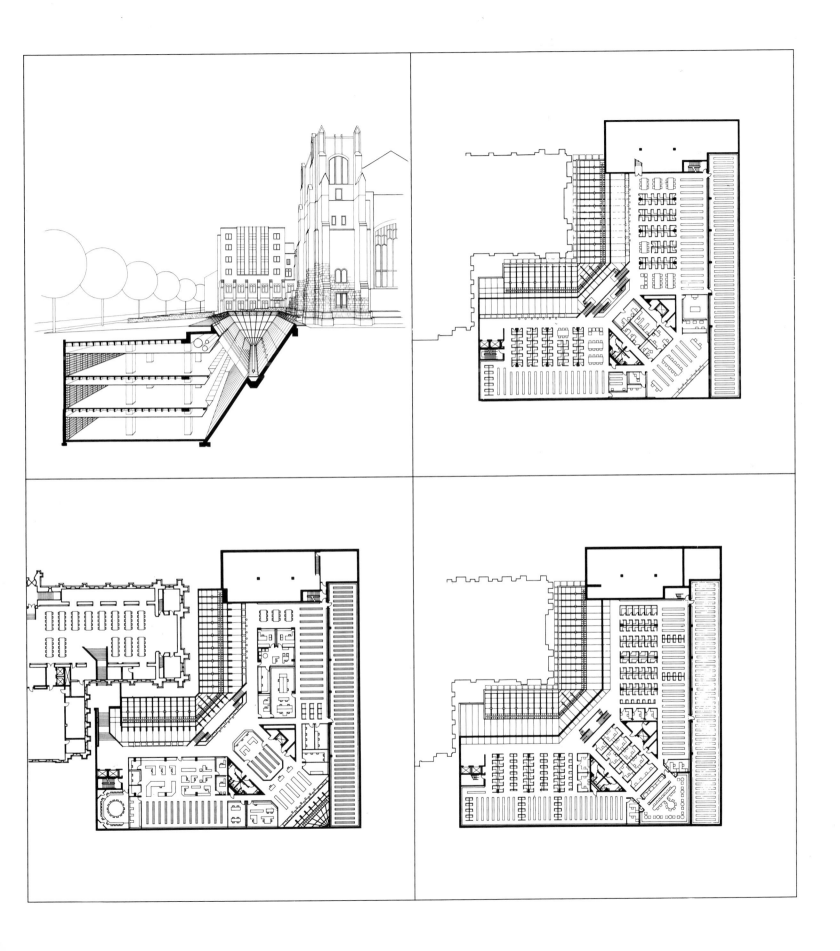

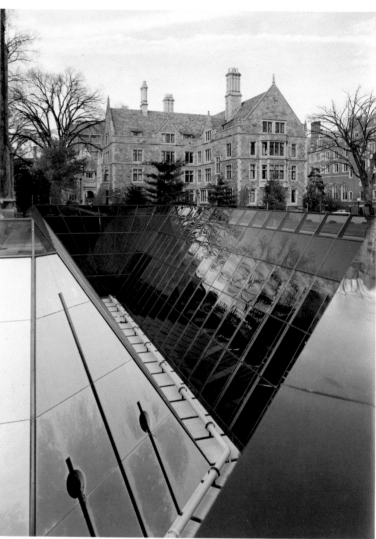

IBM Office Building
Southfield, Michigan, 1974 (1979)

A directive of the program for this building was to conserve energy by every means available. The design incorporates a number of architectural and engineering solutions. A bright aluminum surface on the south and west reflects heat, while a darker gray material on the north and east absorbs heat. The narrow, sloped-glass windows are self-shielding. Interior surfaces are light-colored for reflection. Generated heat from lights, machinery and people is collected, transformed and stored in large water tanks for reuse.

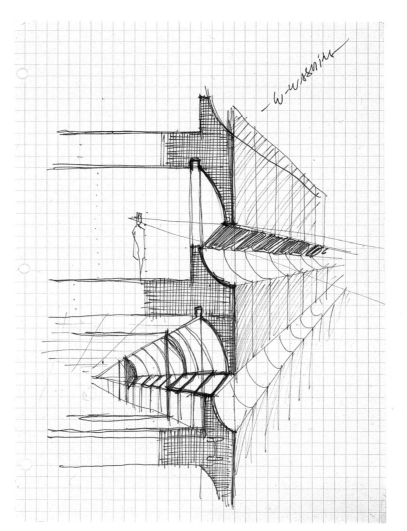

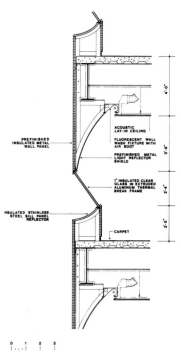

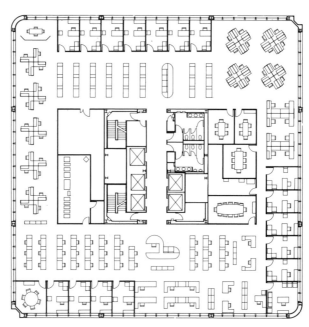

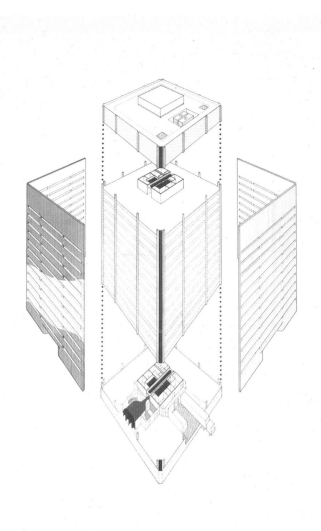

Subterranean Urban Systems Study

Graham Foundation Grant, 1974

Birkerts describes this proposal as "in part a critique of our urban environment which was born from two seeds. One contained conviction and intuition. The other, knowledge and research." The study calls for a radical reform of existing approaches to the use of space in cities, but one not so radical as to require the restructuring of society. Space would be assigned differently: subterranean, surface, and above-ground space would be independently controlled and developed as three distinct layers. At the heart of the concept is the observation that urban lands are not being used effectively. Vestiges of the Industrial Revolution are inhibiting the full potential of city life. Manufacturing plants, warehouses, railroad lines and power plants, along with the mistakes of mid-twentieth century planning – parking lots, service stations and expressways – could be placed underground. The result would be a more orderly environment. Land would be freed for construction of housing, schools, parks and other compatible human uses. Daylight, air and visual awareness of the world above could be brought below ground.

Birkerts' class of graduate students and the Rackham Foundation at the University of Michigan contributed to this study, later published as *Subterranean Urban Systems*. "There are too many individual buildings today," Birkerts and his associates wrote. "Not every physical or functional need deserves the right to become a visual object on our landscape.... We have to impose a 'birth control' upon certain buildings and other structures in order to check the ugliness of urban sprawl."

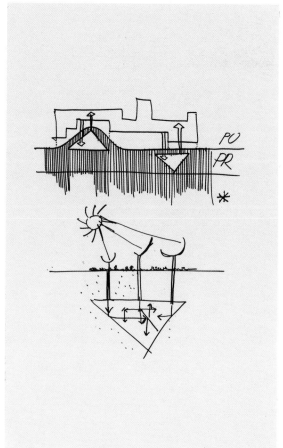

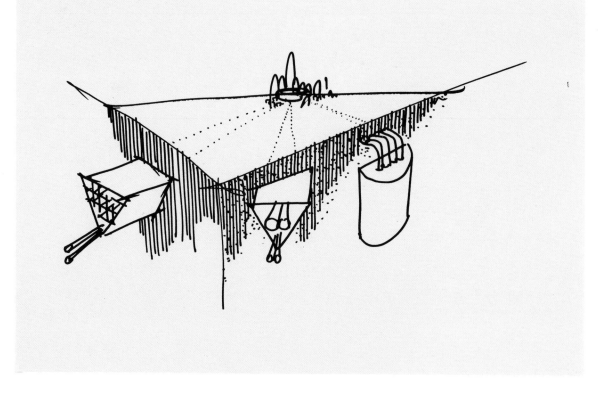

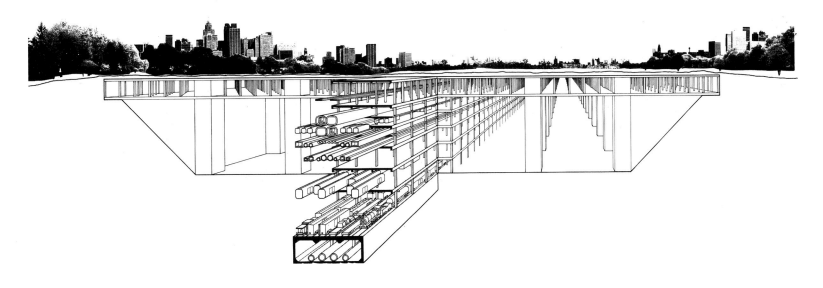

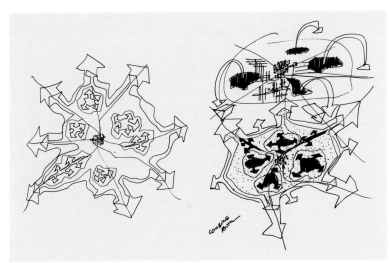

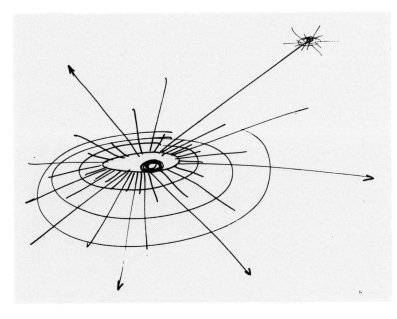

U.S. Embassy

Helsinki, Finland, 1975 (project)

The embassy building blends
Finland's tradition of the strong,
protective, sheltering architecture with
the highly developed building
technologies of the United States.
Scale is broken down by multifaceted
polygonal forms, which bring the
embassy in line with the surrounding
historic architecture.

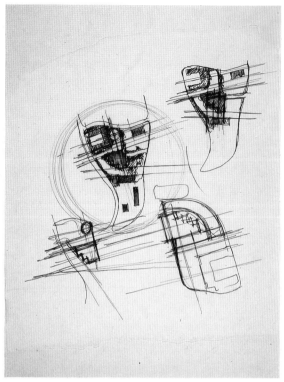

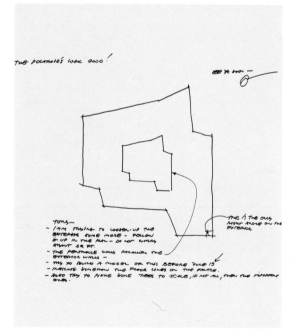

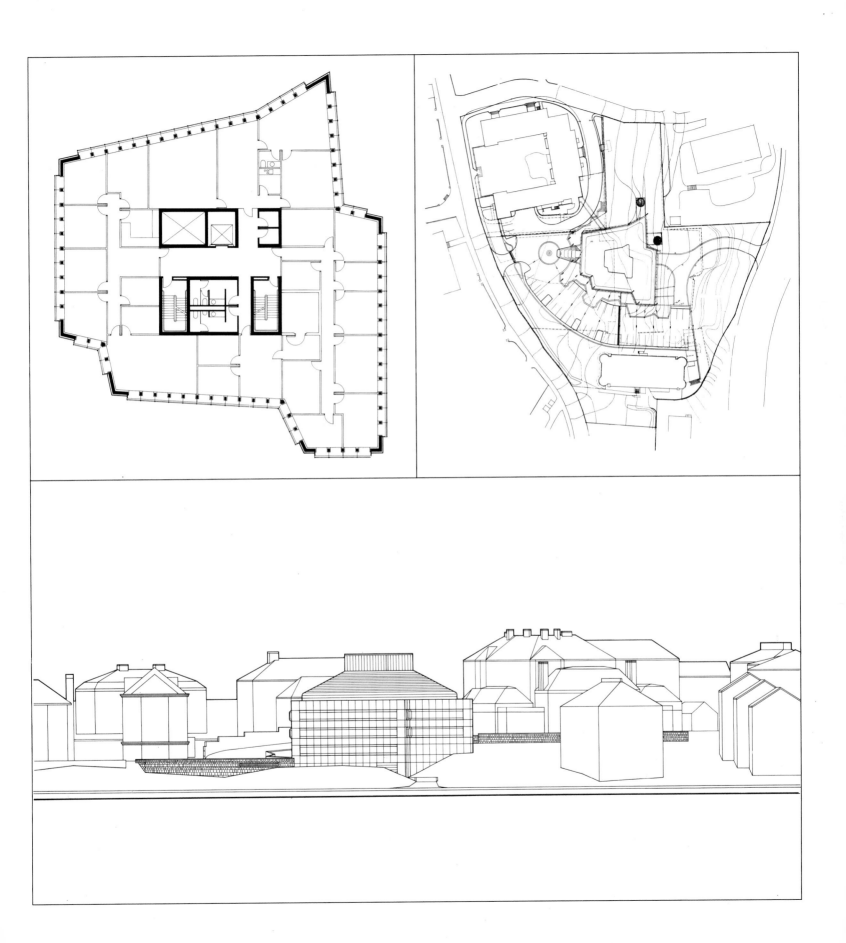

Duluth Public Library
Duluth, Minnesota, 1976 (1980)

The site is narrow and the library is like an anchored ship whose prow points toward the city. The upper floors had to cantilever over public property – a requirement that gives the building's sculptural form a practical basis. The exterior is porcelain steel panels and glass. Inclined glass shields the southern exposure, but a band of silver panels under the windows diffuses the light onto a reflecting panel on the interior.

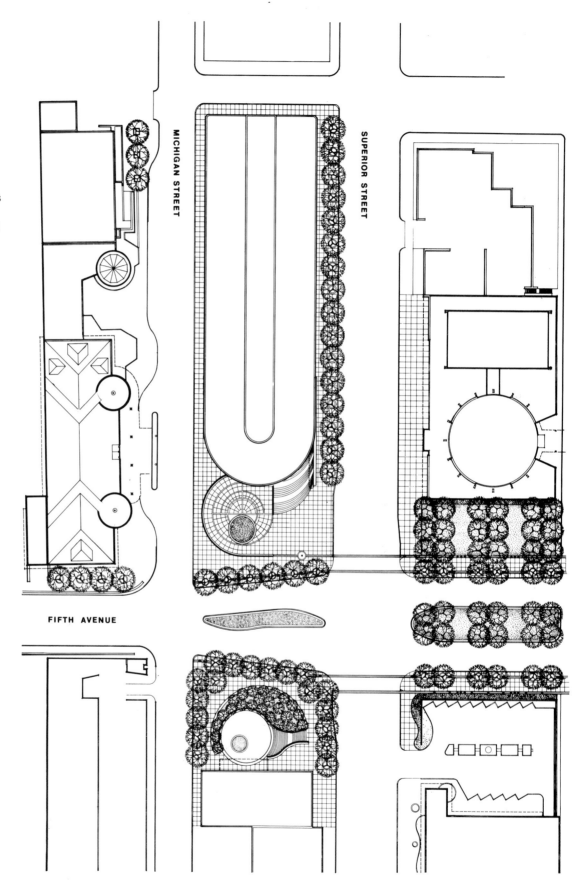

MICHIGAN STREET

SUPERIOR STREET

FIFTH AVENUE

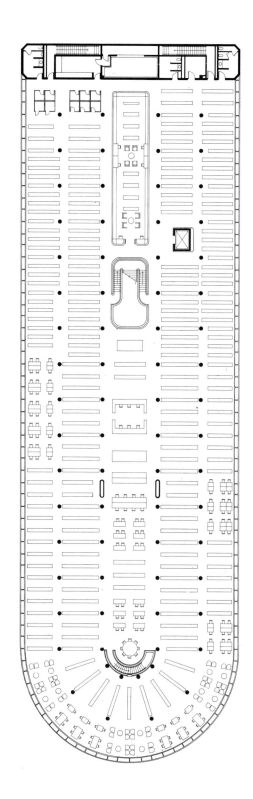
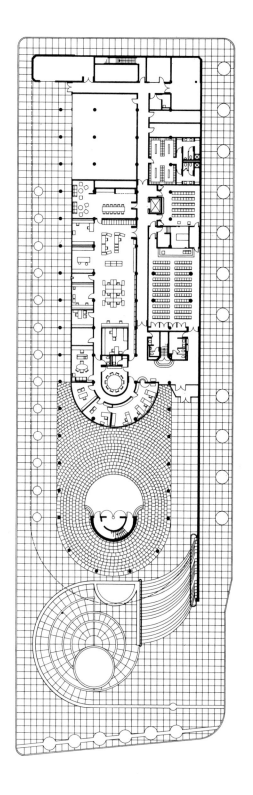

Museum of Glass
Corning, New York, 1976 (1980)

The museum was conceived as a
flowing extension of an existing
building. Its most expressive formal
analogy is to glass itself: an
amorphous material in the molten
state but a highly structured crystal
when solid. The building's exterior
glass has a textured face and is
back–coated with powdered
stainless steel. Daylight comes in
through what Birkerts calls a "linear
periscope" that skirts the perimeter
near the floor.
"[Corning] marks the return of the
didactic approach to technology... an
explosive [Francesco] Borrominian
appendix of orthogonal network
which also evokes the *Glasarchitektur*
of Scheerbart and Taut.... Between
history and utopia there exists an
accessible intermediate area, ...
'patient research'...."
Pasquale Belfiore, *Domus* (October
1981)

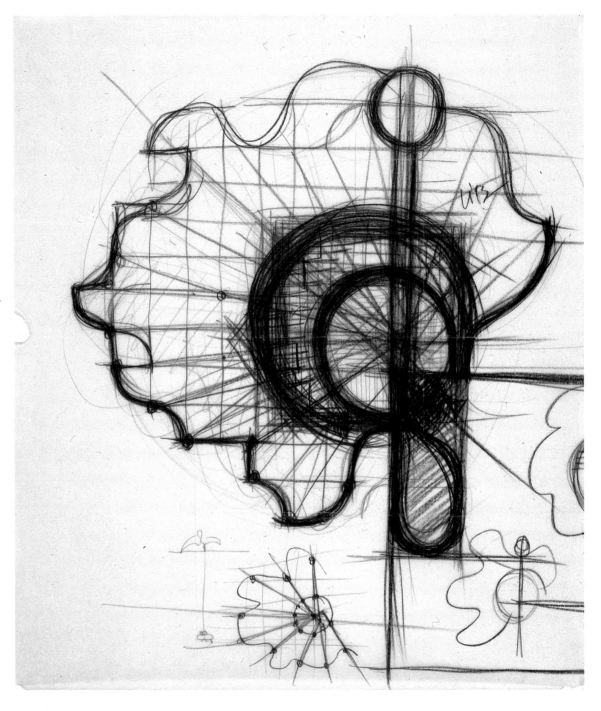

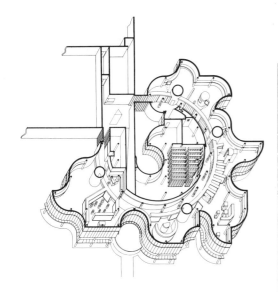

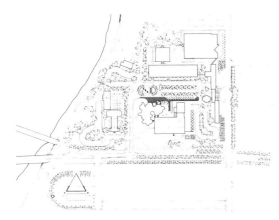

Citrin Office Building

Bingham Farms, Michigan, 1979
(project)

The orthogonal geometry of the planning grid gives this building an essentially square plan. The south side, influenced by the view of a stream, a ravine and abundant trees, develops a faceted edge and opens up in shielded glass.

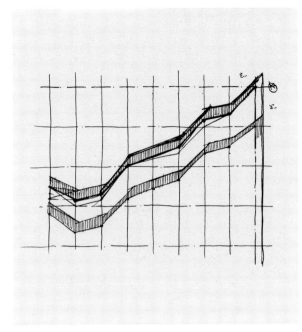

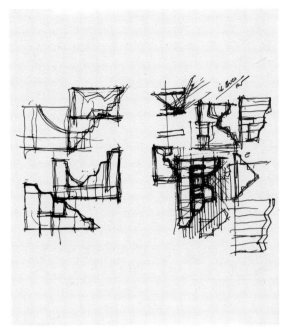

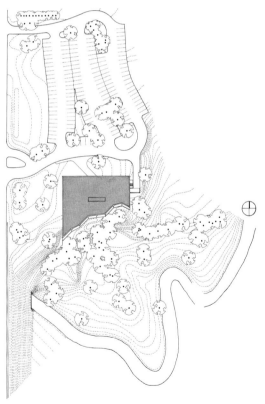

University of Iowa College of Law
Iowa City, Iowa, 1979 (1986)

An articulated, circular form identifies this five-story structure. The circle is pure; it cannot be compromised. It expresses perfection and integrity, and suggests concentration, study and seclusion.

The materials – limestone for the skin, metal trim on the exterior and wood on the interior – are native. The structure is earthbound yet full of light.

The central cylinder contains the main vertical circulation elements and is also a major solar collector. The dome's height and bulk are subordinated to the nearby state capitol, yet it asserts itself in this region where a dome signals an important cultural building.

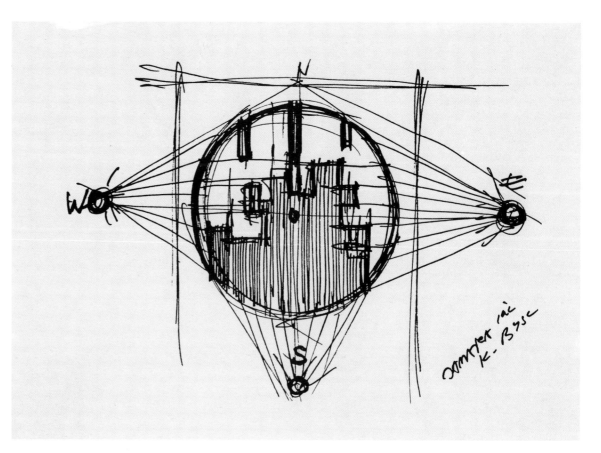

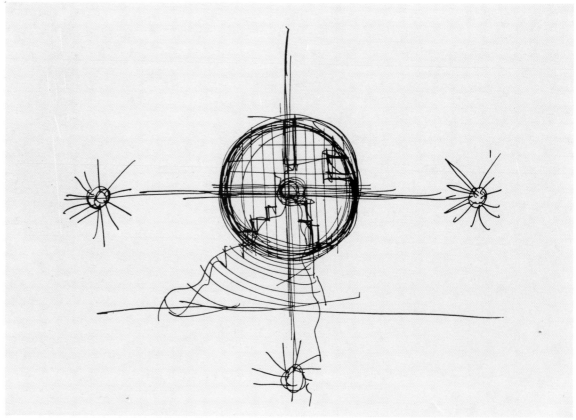

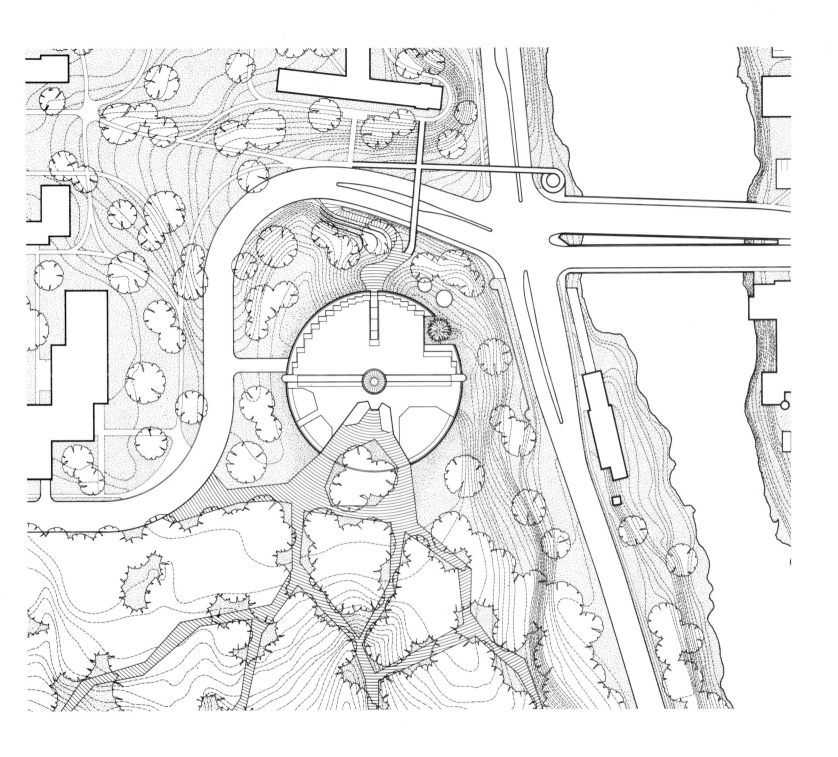

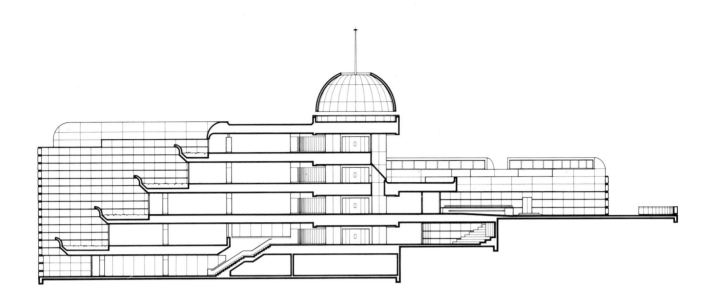

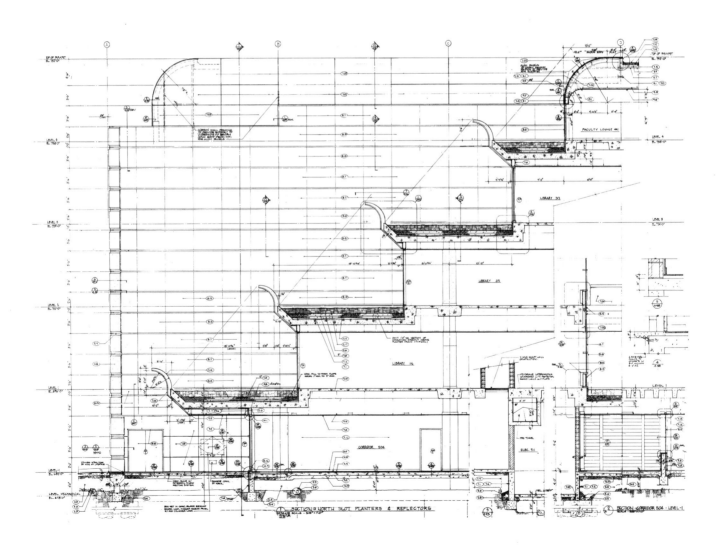

SECTION NORTH SLOT PLANTERS & REFLECTORS

SECTION CORRIDOR 504 LEVEL-1

Cathedral of the Most Blessed Sacrament Renovation
Detroit, Michigan, 1980 (project)

The new parish space for the cathedral was designed as a gentle, flowing space that was inserted into the existing rigid Gothic order. The new does not touch the old. The new space rises dynamically, like a scroll edged in marble and wood that proclaims the congregation's faith.

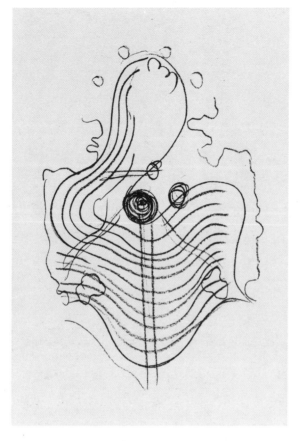

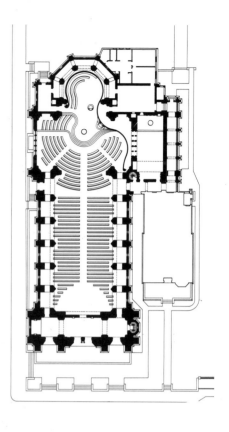

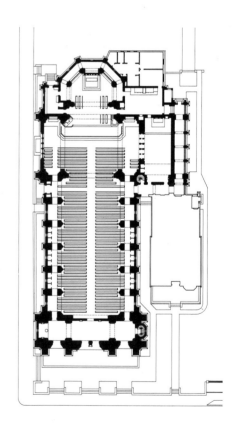

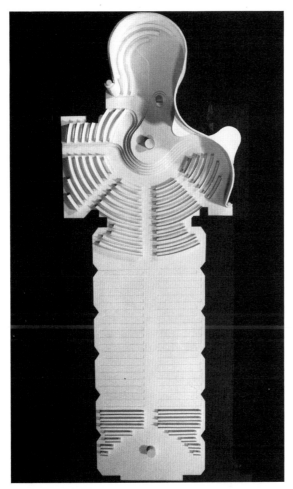

Ferguson Residence ("Villa Ginny")

Kalamazoo, Michigan, 1980 (1983)

Outside, this house is an organic form, moving with nature on all six sides. Inside, the built order projects through the roof, light scoops, chimneys and exhausts.

Two concepts were working here: The core of the house is orthogonal to accommodate the functions. Its basic form is the right angle. But this core is prevented from connecting directly to the organically segmented exterior wall by a sliding panel. "Like an organic growth, the building has a skin and also a core," says the architect. Teak, stucco and copper are the materials.

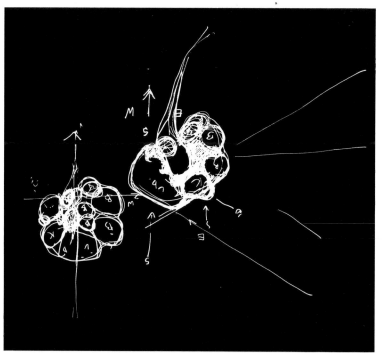
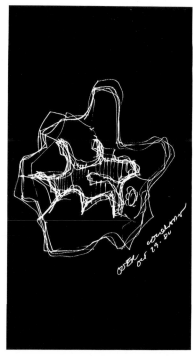
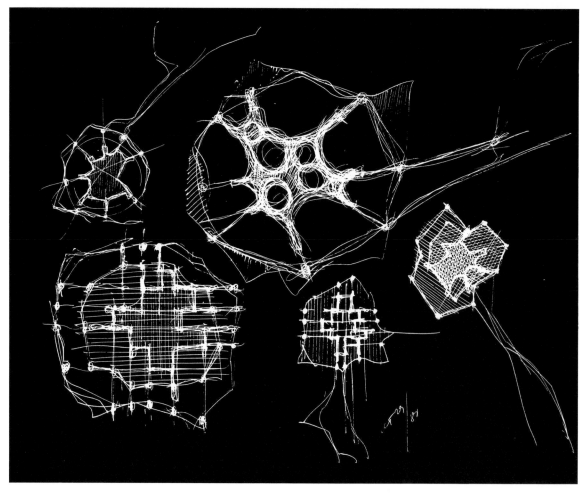

118

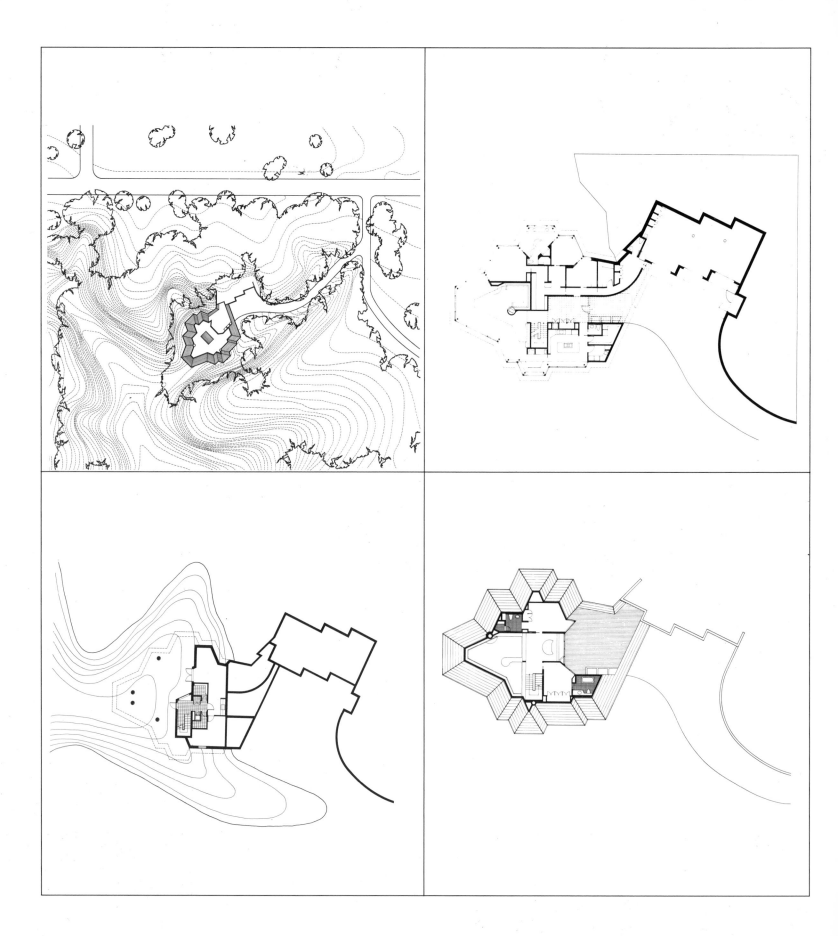

Cornell University
Uris Library Addition
Ithaca, New York, 1980 (1982)

This earth-covered reading room is
an addition to a Richardsonian
Romanesque undergraduate library.
The building is lighted by daylight
and has views of the grounds. Earth
was moved to enhance the existing
building visually.

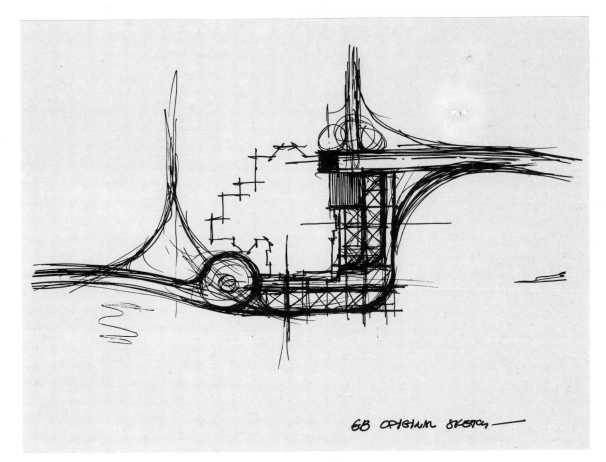

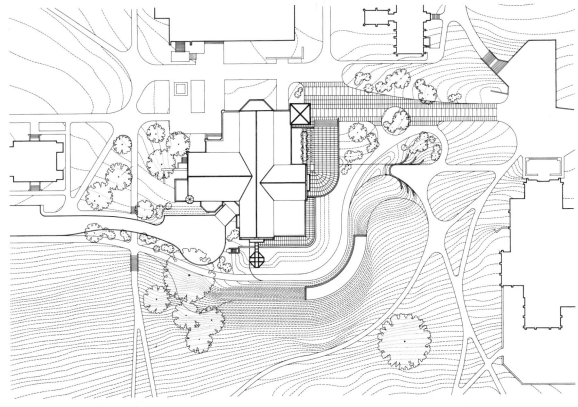

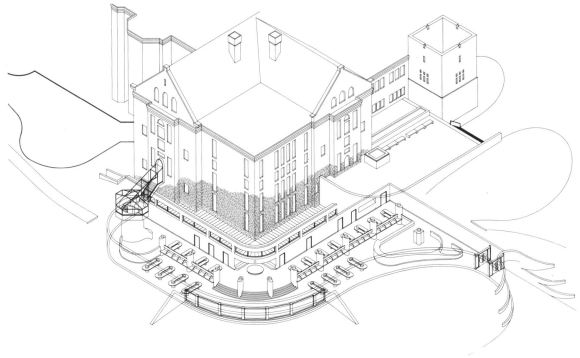

St. Peter's Lutheran Church
Columbus, Indiana, 1980 (1988)

The Nordic/Germanic Protestant
heritage of the congregation
influenced the design of this
1,000-seat church. Its geometry and
form suggest a duality of opposites:
the orthogonal and the curvilinear
meet suddenly, as they do in life.
Concrete, brick and copper are the
materials. The interior is designed to
accommodate the congregation on
rising levels and to control natural
light. The sanctuary is finished in
white plaster with pews and trim in
natural maple.

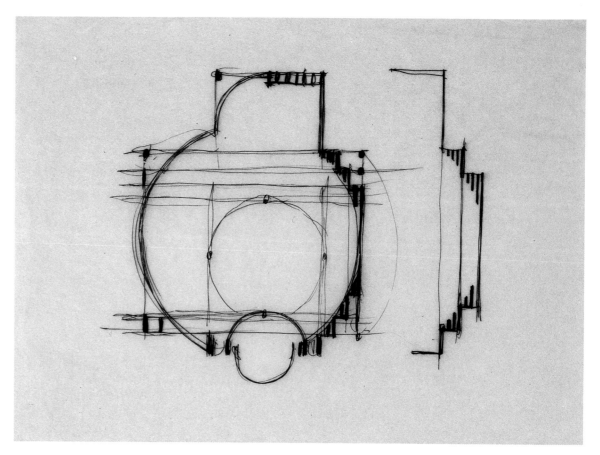

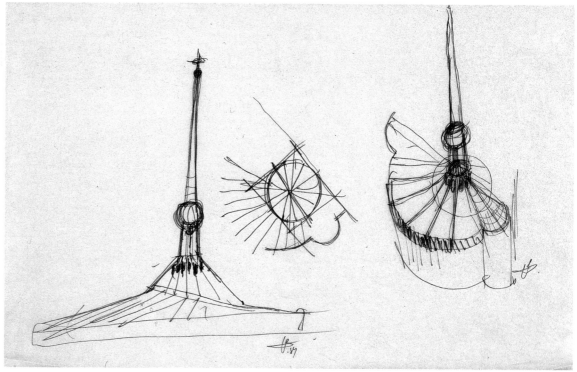

124

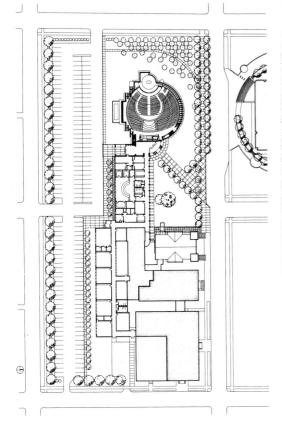

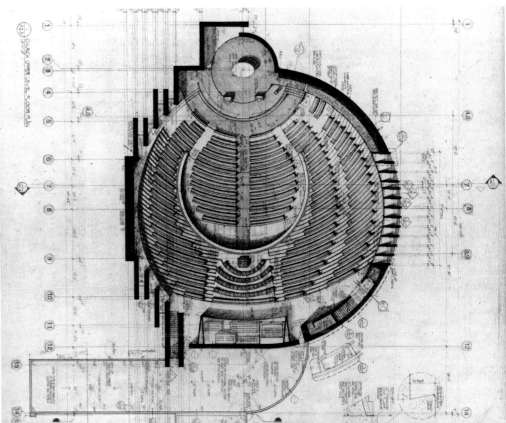

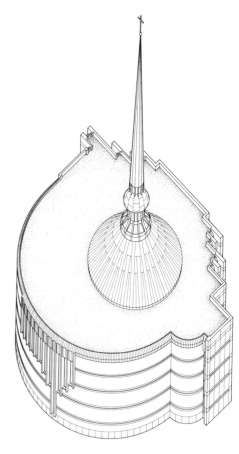

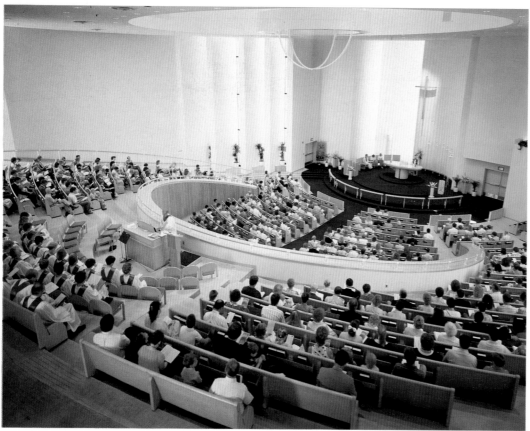

State of Wisconsin Office Building
Green Bay, Wisconsin, 1981 (1983)

This building's form clearly expresses
the passive energy design concepts.
It turns its face to the south as
broadly as possible, reaching for
warmth and light in this cold climate.
The use of passive energy also
determines the elevation design.

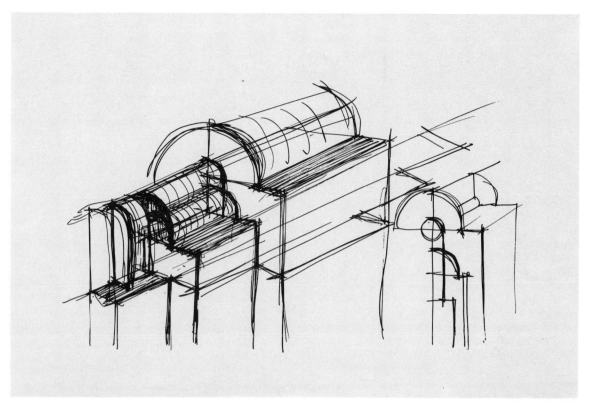

Anchorage Library Competition
Anchorage, Alaska, 1981 (project)

The form of this design is generated by the strong influence of the orientation, climate and views to the surrounding landscape. "There was no vernacular to speak of – nothing to allude to, or relate to – so you look at nature for the outside influence, and then you look at the function inside that you have to perform," says the architect. Extended bays toward the south respond to climatic influences to produce a practical passive solar design and Birkerts' signature – extraordinary interior daylighting. The glass sphere atop the central light well reflects daylight into the interior and symbolizes the quest for knowledge – the head, the mind, the sun.

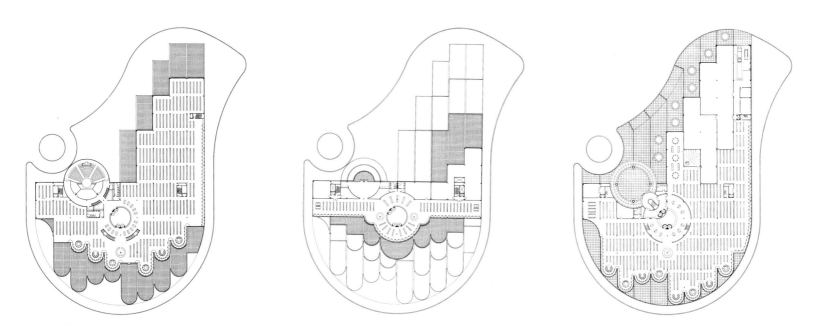

Holtzman & Silverman
Office Building
Southfield, Michigan, 1983 (1989)

This building provides a very
personal 2,600-square-foot office
space for two highly cultured
businessmen and art devotees. The
program included premium office
space and systems to house major
art and book collections.
The narrow, one-acre site was
restrictive; municipal codes
generated a scheme that sent the
building partially into the hillside and
the parking to the roof. The
landscaped surface to the west is
mounded to obscure nearby
commercial development. The
metaphor is a cave filled with light:
the scheme incorporates reinforced
concrete retaining walls, exposed
aggregate at the entry tower and on
the ravine facade and an entry area
clad in granite and polished stainless
steel infilled with glass. A generous
overhang and planters reduce glare
and heat gain.

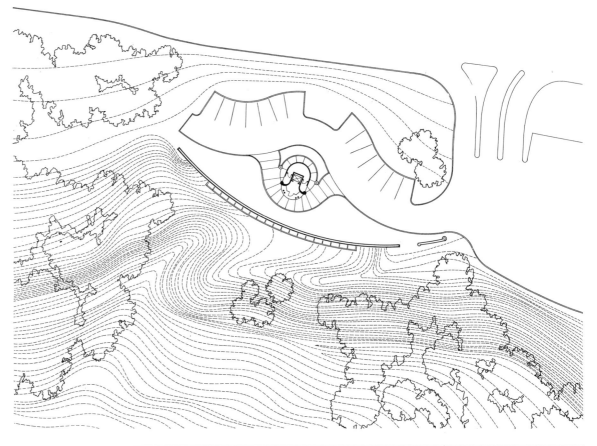

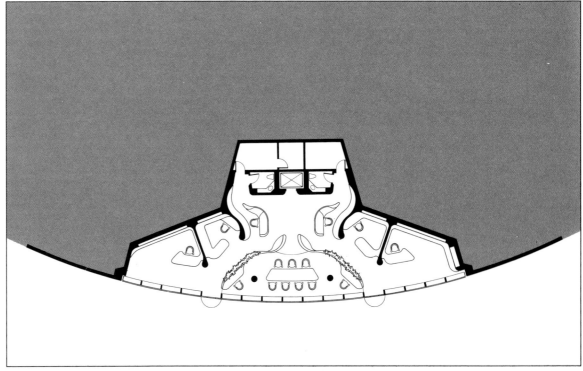

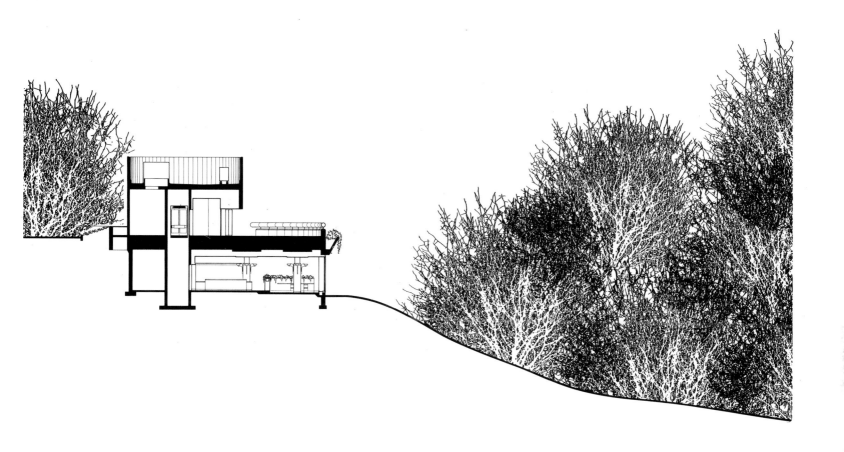

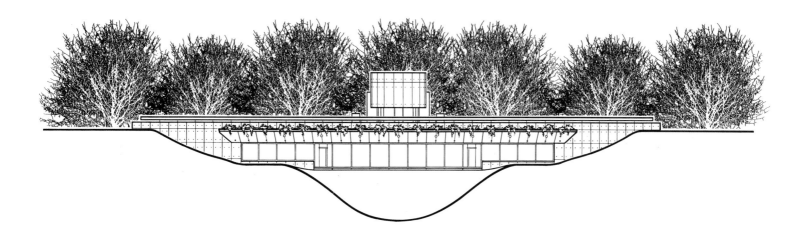

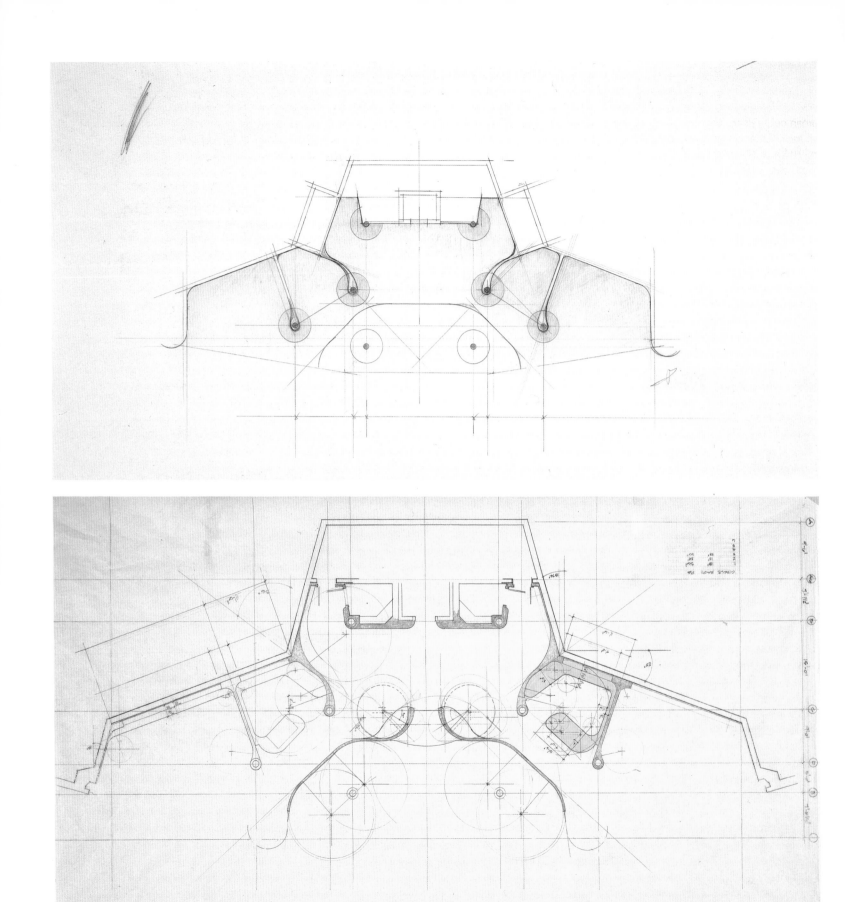

Woodbranch Energy Plaza
Houston, Texas, 1982 (project)

Birkerts calls this a "self-contained urban cell." Office, commercial and recreational space are contained within the sinuous master plan, designed to accommodate change and adaption over a ten-year development.

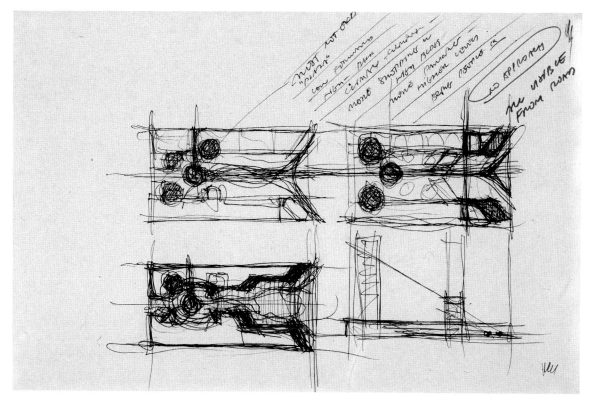

Domino's Farms Master Plan
Ann Arbor, Michigan, 1984

This program required enormous amounts of space but was hindered by a four-story height regulation. Hence this dynamic, linear concept emerged. "The organic land form and the man-made structure interface; the linear is penetrated by the organic. The surrounding road network and parking areas conform to the organic planning and landscaping concept," says the architect.

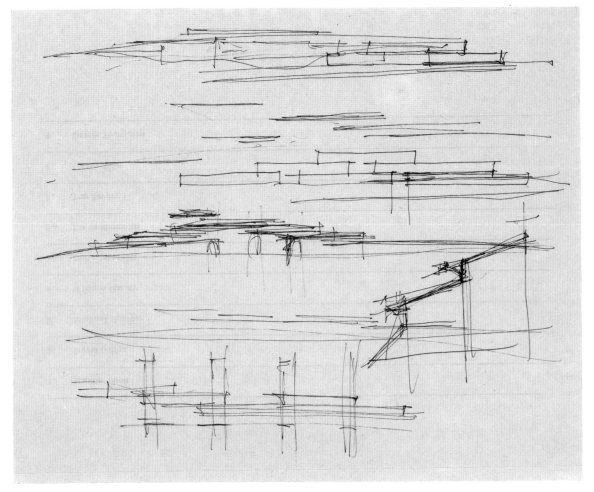

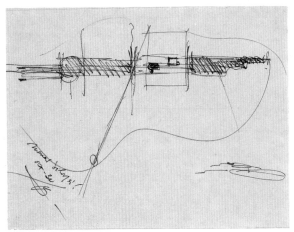

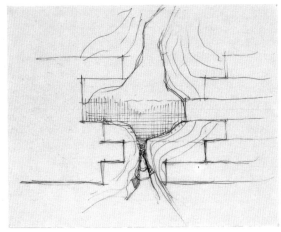

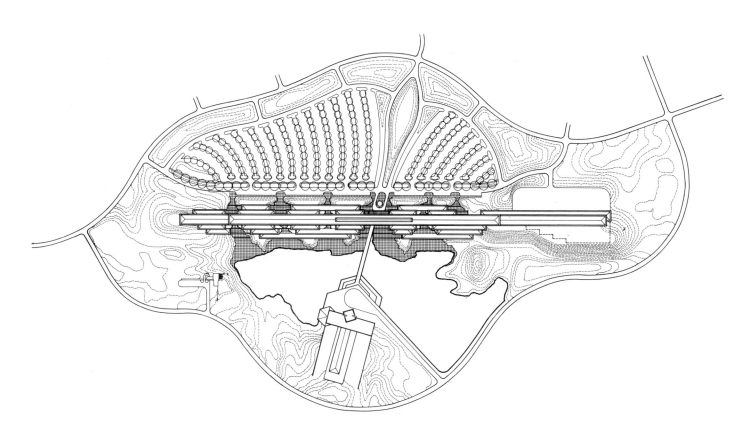

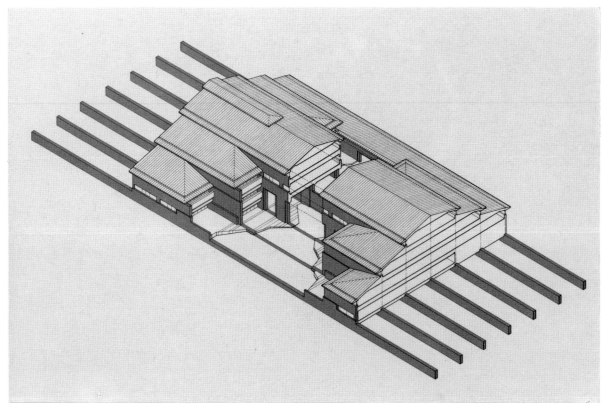

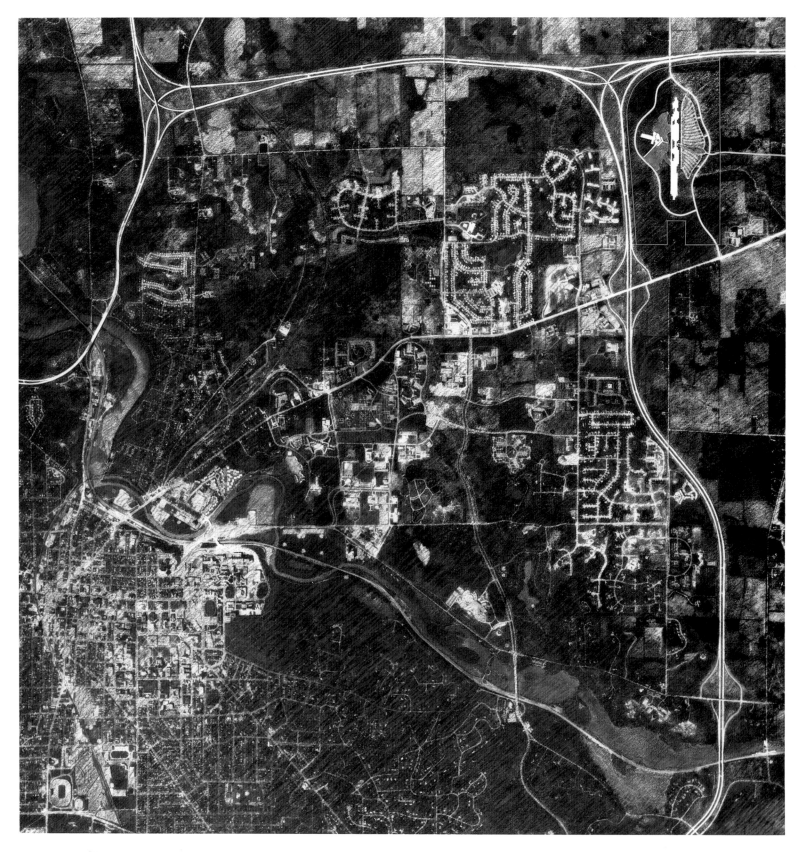

138

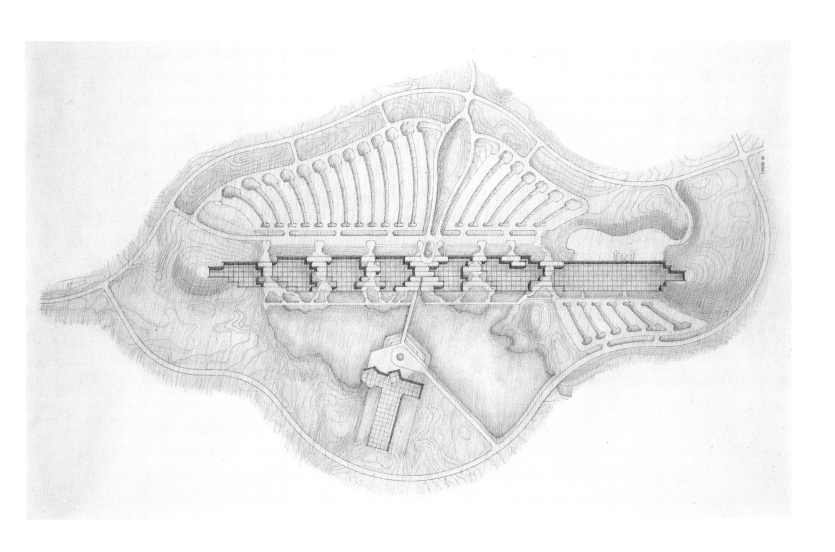

Domino's Pizza, Inc.
Headquarters
Ann Arbor, Michigan, 1984
(in progress)

The seven "tracks" in this design vary
from one to four stories to produce a
volumetrically expandable space
container. The architect had to solve
the requirements of office space,
warehousing, test kitchens, a
museum and recreational areas.
These uses had to be contained
within a form that met certain
requirements of the client: the
complex had to be immediately
identifiable from the adjacent
expressway and contain references
to the client's hero, Frank Lloyd
Wright. Birkerts did what Wright
would have done in similar
circumstances. He did not imitate but
approached the problem based on
site, climate and client need, with a
view to the century to come.

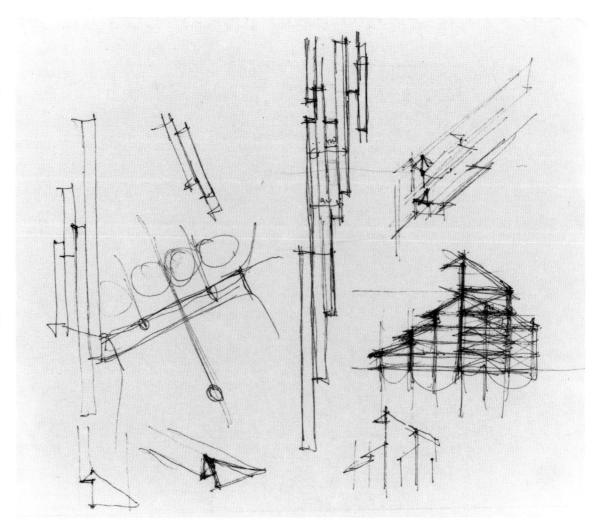

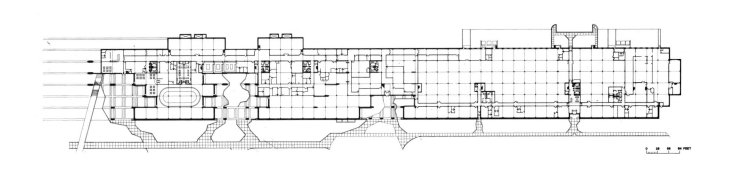

0 28 56 84 FEET

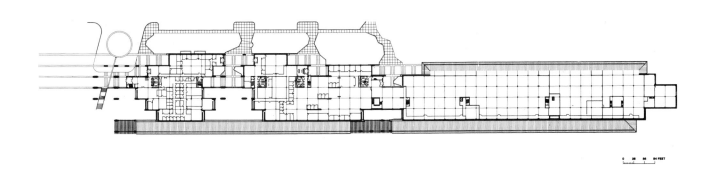

0 28 56 84 FEET

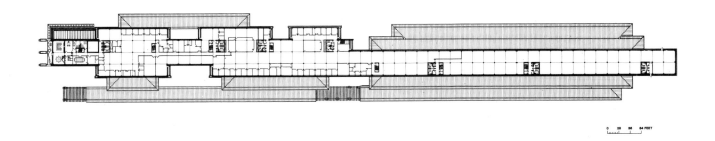

0 28 56 84 FEET

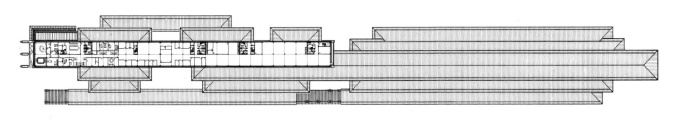

0 28 56 84 FEET

Minnesota Judicial Building Competition

St. Paul, Minnesota, 1984 (project)

The existing building is an excellent expression of governmental dignity. The objective was to design an addition that enhanced the older structure rather than overwhelmed it. Mimicry of the existing neoclassical architecture was out of the question. The concept proposed a background building, carefully subordinated to the adjoining monuments.

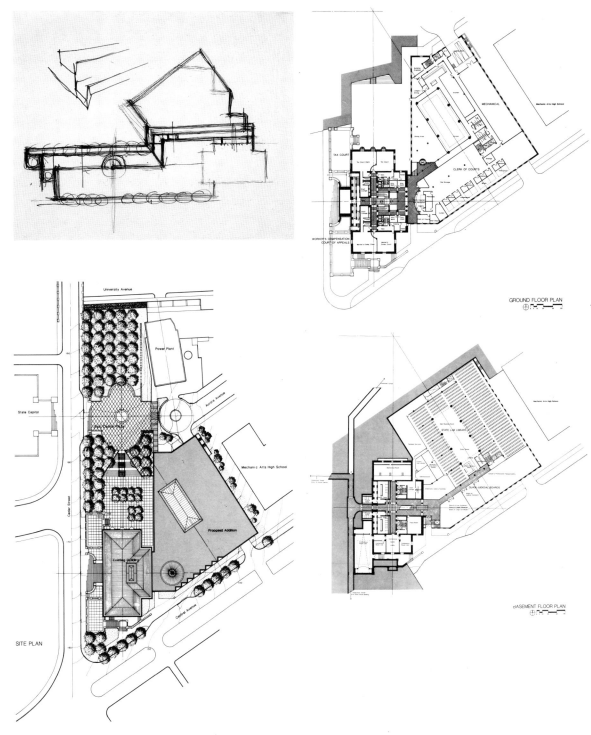

GROUND FLOOR PLAN

SITE PLAN

BASEMENT FLOOR PLAN

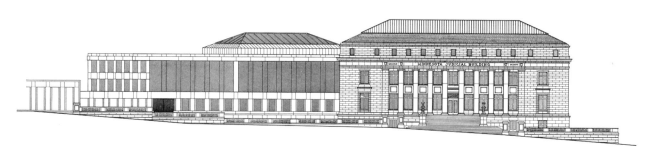

WEST

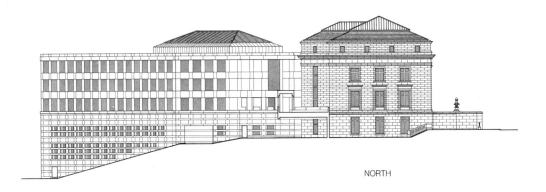

NORTH

Minnesota History Center Competition

St. Paul, Minnesota, 1984 (project)

This triangular container encloses a single space whose upper four levels do not touch the exterior wall plane. Work spaces are placed on the periphery of the core triangle. The points of the triangle are directed toward views of Cass Gilbert's state capitol, St. Paul's cathedral and the center of St. Paul.

The enclosing walls convey strength and permanence. Metaphorically, the wall section rises from the geological base and attenuates as it reaches for the light. Perforations through the wall light the interior circulation space and allow for vision and awareness of the exterior surroundings from the balcony. Terraced levels create people spaces on the exterior that are sheltered by cascading terraces and indigenous vegetation. The symbols in the landscape design recall Minnesota's prairies, mountains, and lakes and waterways.

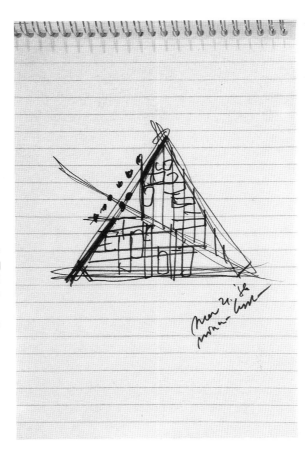

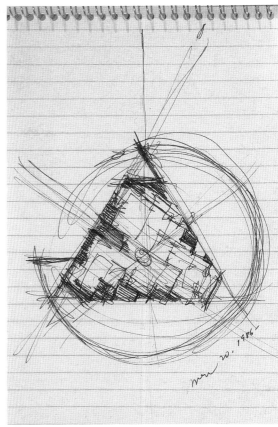

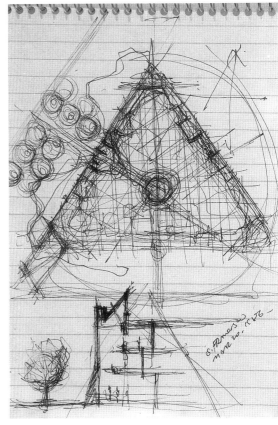

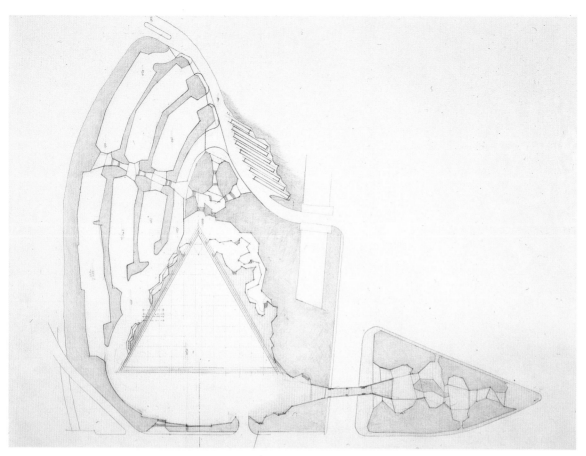

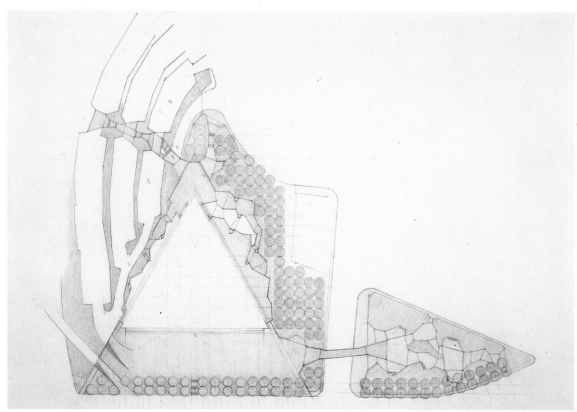

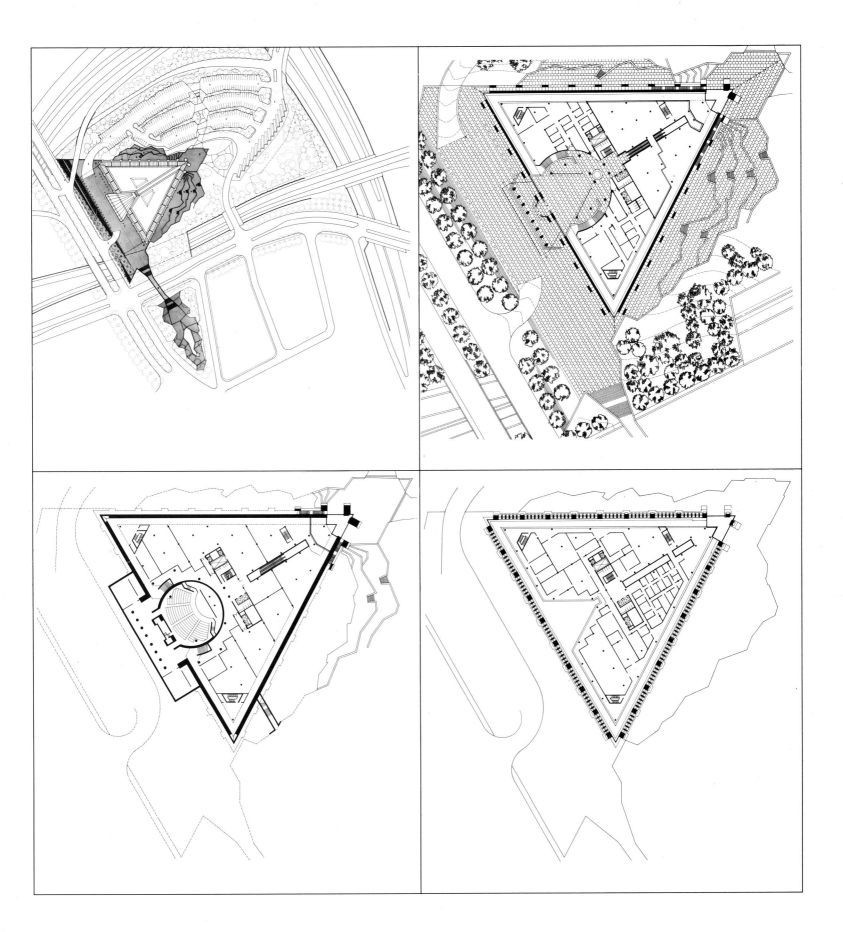

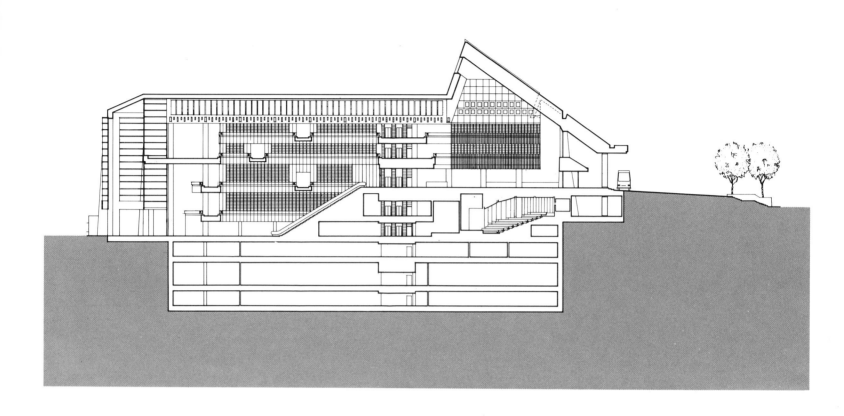

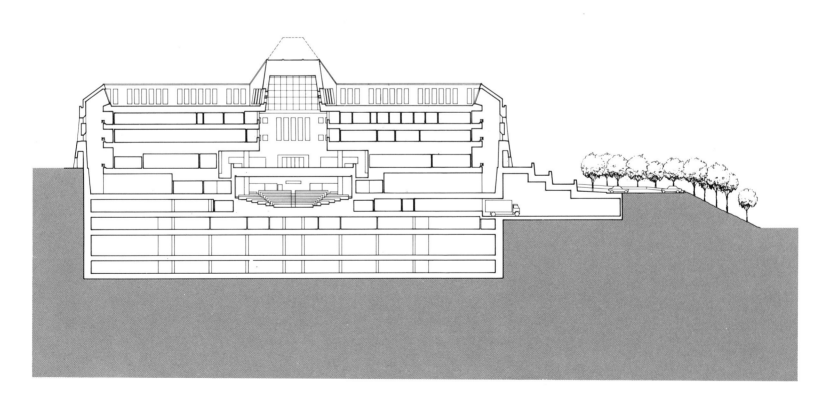

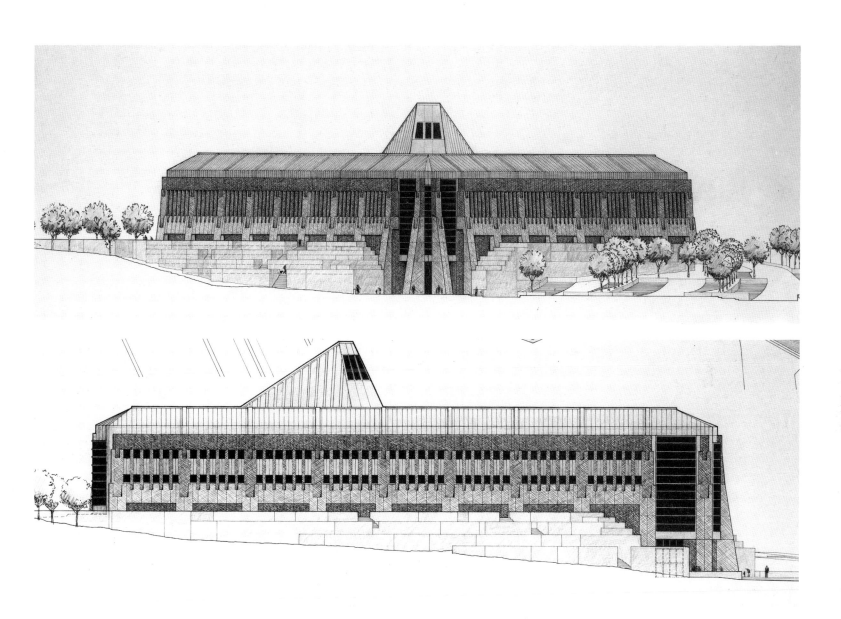

149

Bardha Residence
Birmingham, Michigan, 1984 (1989)

This design is strongly influenced by its suburban, small town context and by the client's desire to incorporate Moslem architectural references. The interior is primarily white plaster and wood. The exterior walls are white brick and stucco. The roof fasciae, window shields and chimney are trimmed in black-painted metal and the sloped roof is asphalt shingles, the whole forming a strong black-and-white graphic image.

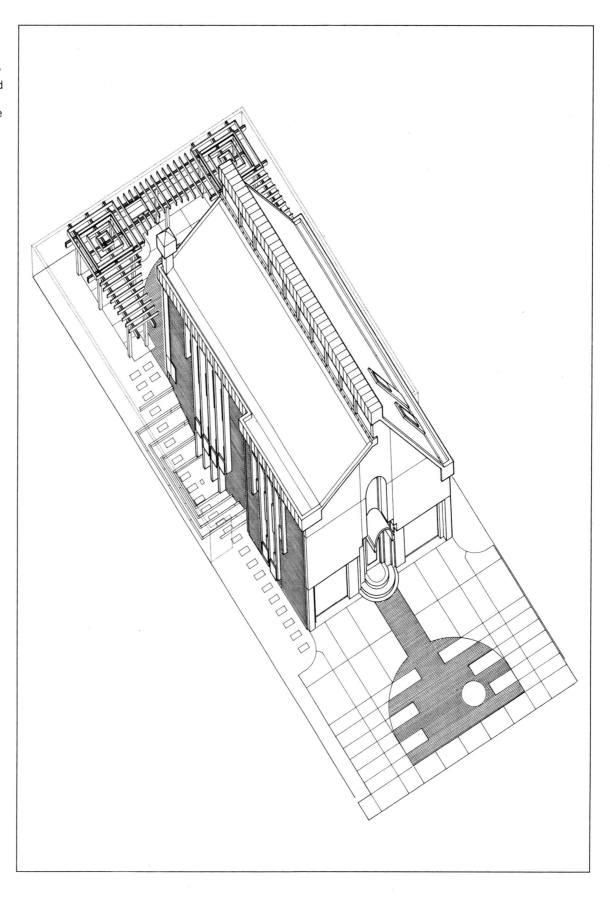

Law School Feasibility Study

Duke University, Durham, North Carolina, 1985

This design solution proposed the expansion of the existing Duke University Law School and an image change for the entire edifice. The design approach is influenced by the school's mix of Georgian, Colonial and collegiate Gothic styles. Birkerts describes the scheme as "a unique visual personality which stands apart from the myriad of influences surrounding it..., a truly eclectic answer."

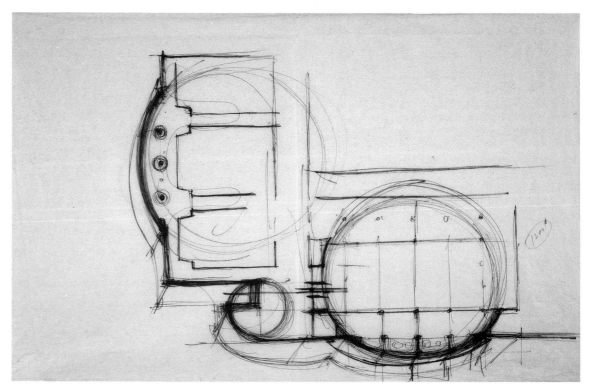

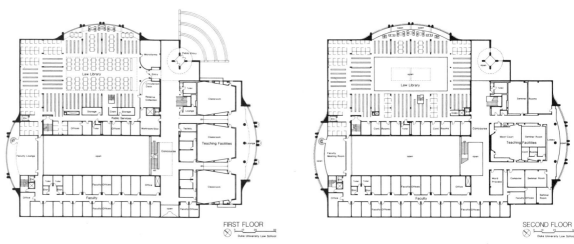

FIRST FLOOR
Duke University Law School

SECOND FLOOR
Duke University Law School

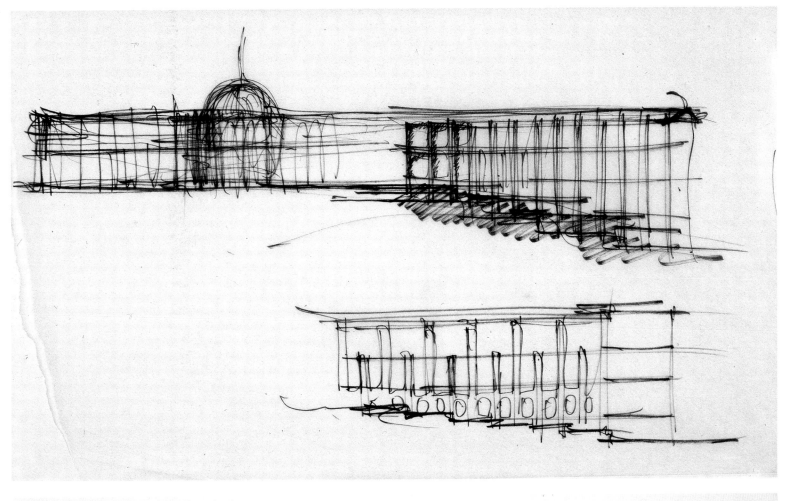

Domino's Pizza, Inc., Special Designs

Ann Arbor, Michigan, 1985 (1986)

The appointments in the executive suite and chairman's quarters are part of the organic whole of the Domino's master plan of 1984. The "tracks" concept, the proportions, the combination of wood and metals and the linearity of the plan are repeated here.

Special designs include a toilet/washroom "module» (p. 156), a candelabrum that incorporates the "tracks" motif (p. 157), a logo for dinnerware and linens (p. 158, top left), a light pedestal and a cigarette urn (p. 158, bottom left), and a firewood carrier (p. 158, right).

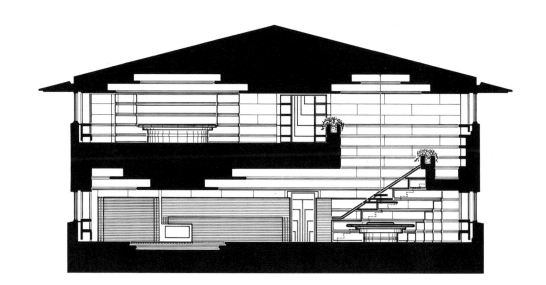

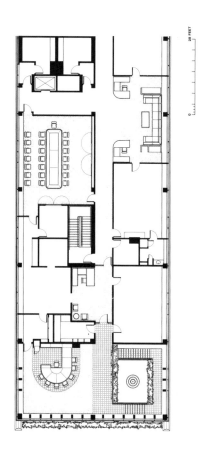

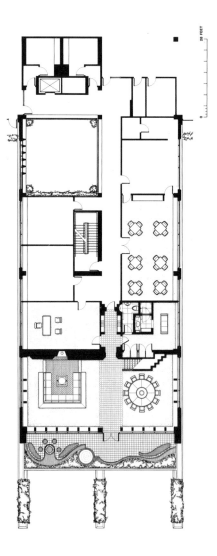

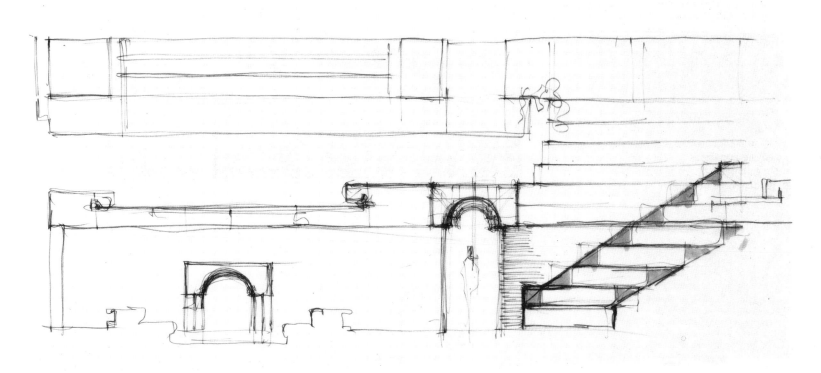

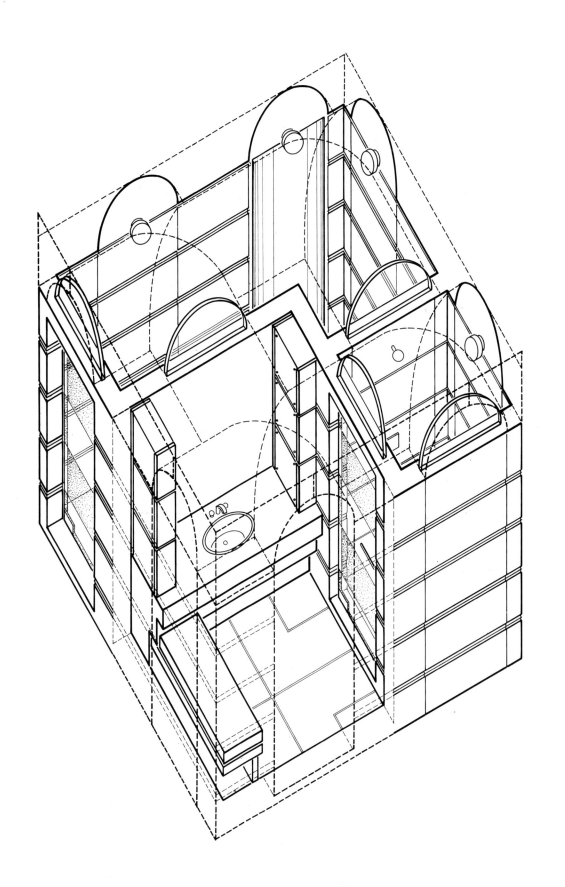

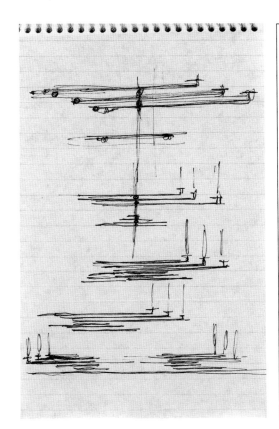

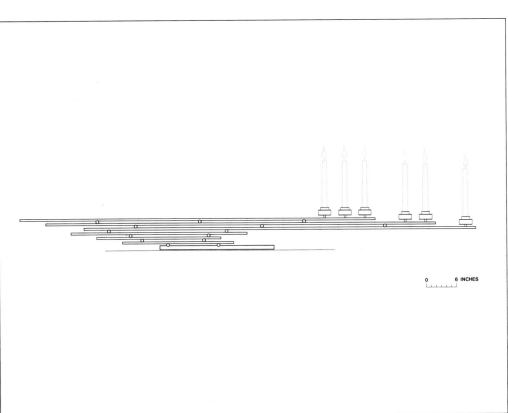

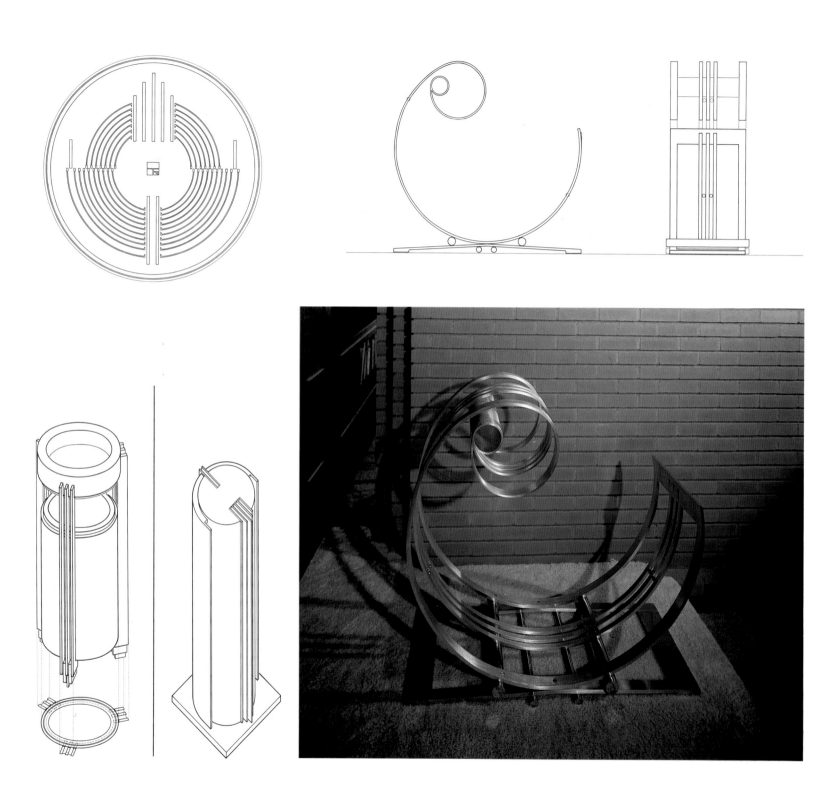

158

Conservatory of Music Library Addition

Oberlin College, Oberlin, Ohio, 1986
(1988)

This concept is an organic response to interior space needs and to context. The building seeks visual continuity with the existing Minoru Yamasaki white quartz aggregate precast concrete structure it is squeezed next to. A Georgian-style church is on the other side.
The proposed building is clad in white tile. Exterior walls make several "inflections," which suggest a relationship with the existing Yamasaki structure. The new building on the block respectfully shifts its position slightly to allow the venerable old one room to breathe. The inflections also visually diminish the length of the wall. Openings in the recesses provide views into the library. The projected light scoop on top brings northeast light into the two-story lounge at the prow.

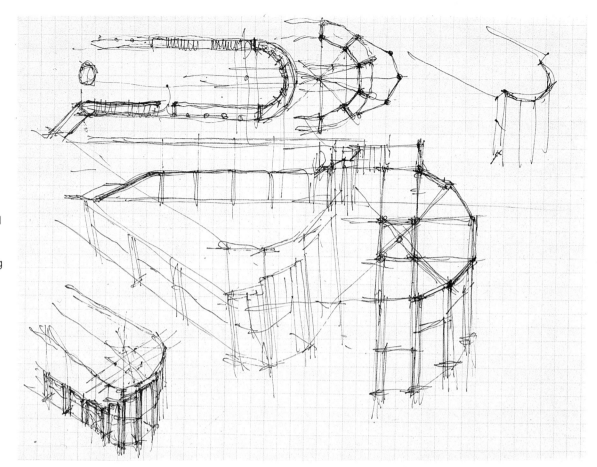

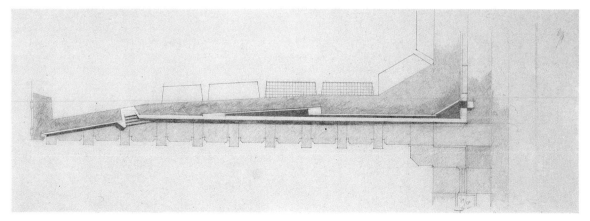

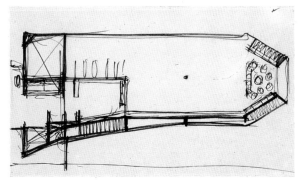

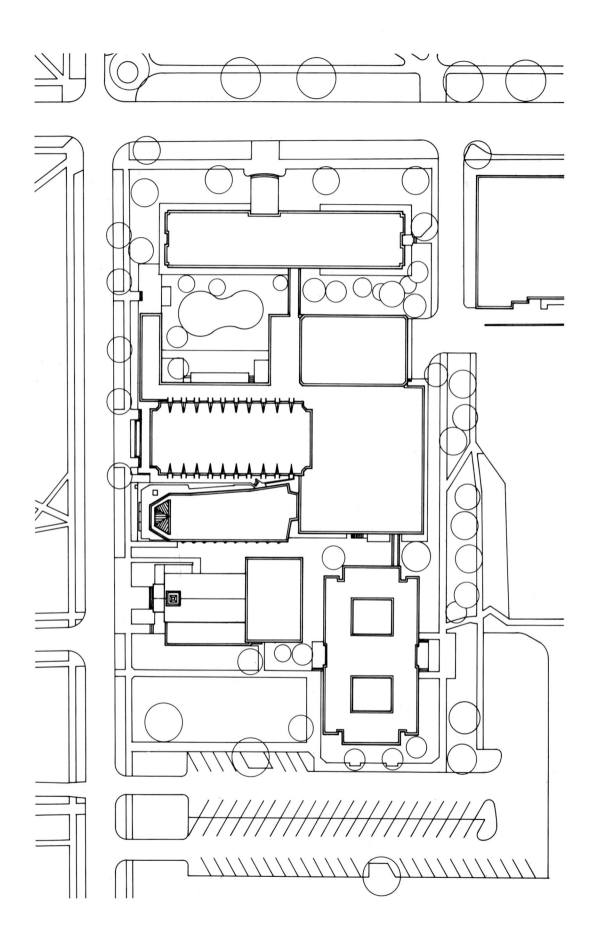

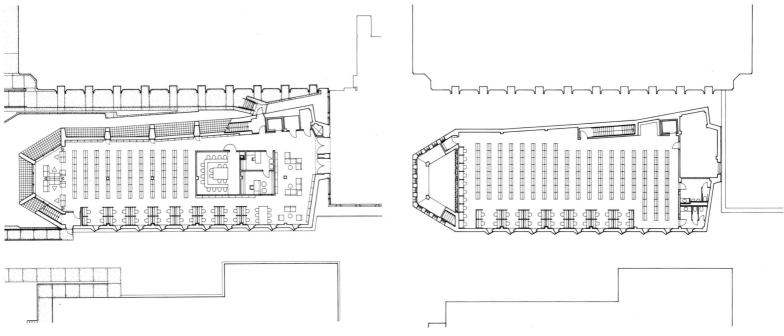

161

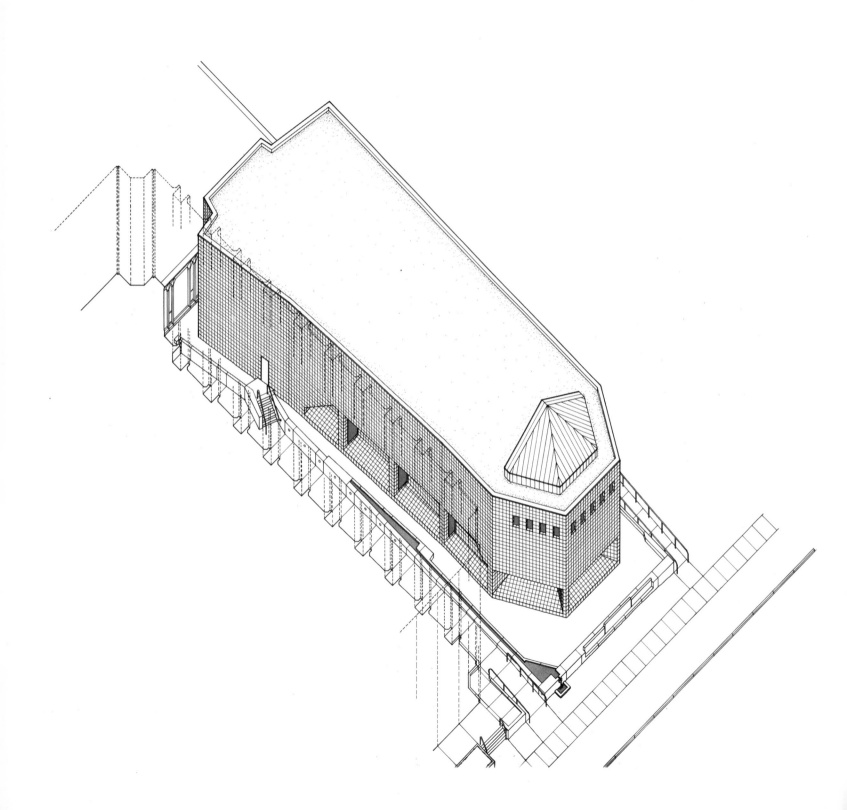

Domino's Pizza, Inc., Prototype Franchise Building
Jackson, Michigan, 1986 (1988)

This pizza sales outlet is also an advertising billboard that playfully announces its identity on the street as a piece of pizza being lifted from the whole. Since the structure had to be easily buildable from common materials, the design calls for block walls, aluminum framing systems and corrugated, galvanized steel panels.

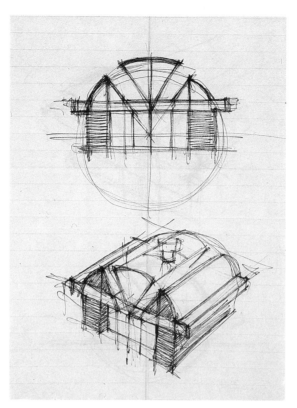

Residence

San Francisco, California, 1986
(project)

This house is sited high on a hilltop overlooking San Francisco and the bay. The floor plan was determined by the client's lifestyle, while the exterior form responds to the natural environment with abrupt changes in level and plane. The silhouette of the house is similar to the form of the mountain on which it sits. Exterior materials are primarily glass and stucco under an expansive copper roof.

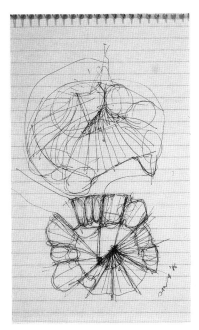
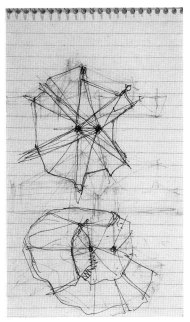
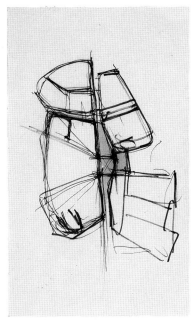

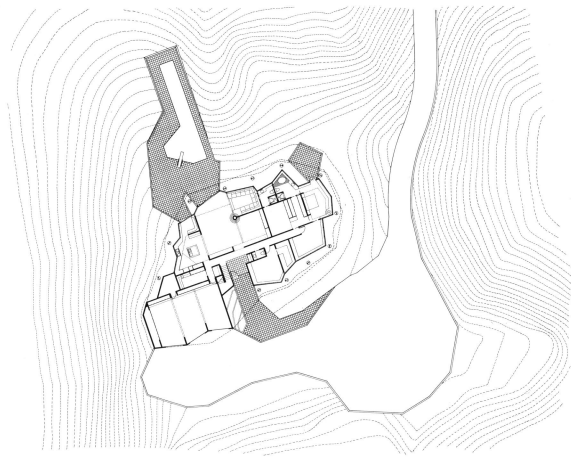

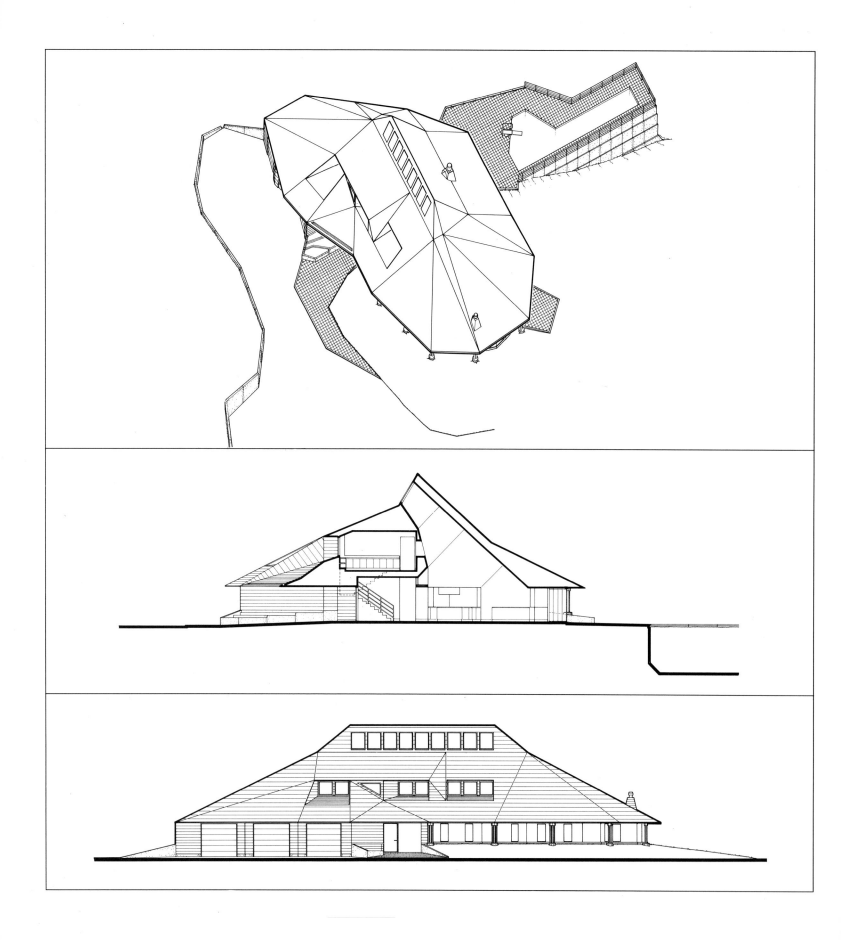

Museum Competition, University of Wyoming

Laramie, Wyoming, 1986 (project)

This proposed museum building and its site plan incorporate references to the Wyoming landscape. The green island surrounding the building is a free-flowing organic form with foot trails cut through indigenous vegetation. The circular colonnade and pergola "corral" the building and identify its place in the vast Wyoming landscape.

The roof expresses the land forms on the horizon, alluding to the Teton mountain range and the lifting of the geological plate that formed it. Birkerts calls this thinking "poetic pragmatism": the combining of a poetic, metaphorical exterior and a pragmatic, efficiently functioning interior.

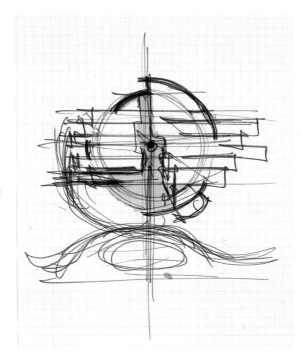

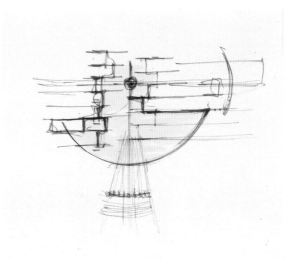

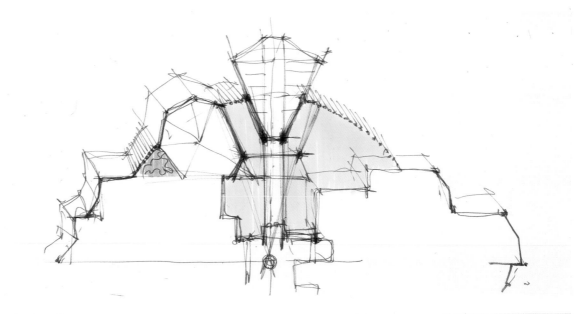

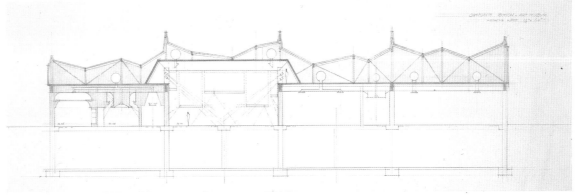

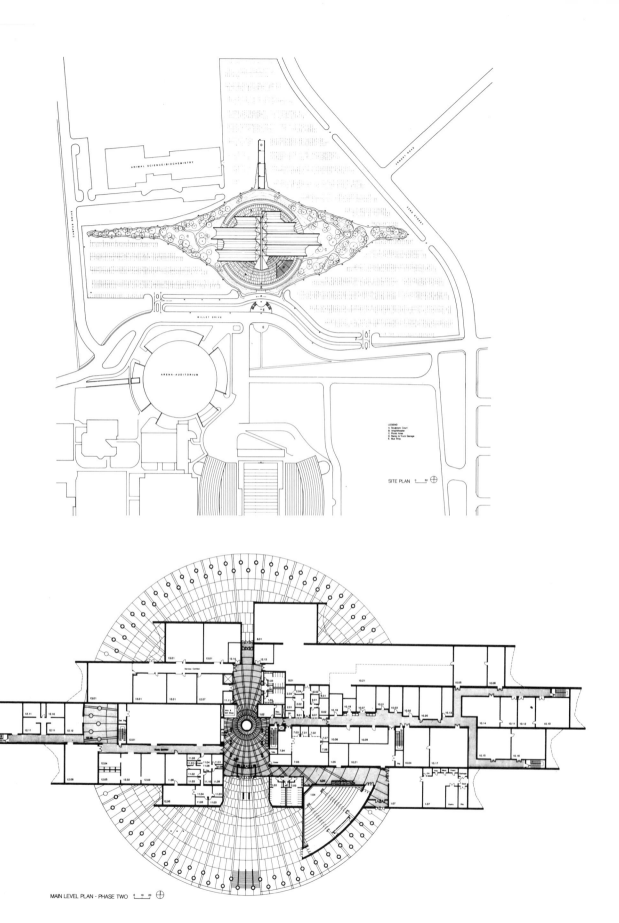

SITE PLAN

MAIN LEVEL PLAN - PHASE TWO

Library Addition, University of California

San Diego, California, 1987
(in progress)

University of California officials
wanted this library addition to be
subordinate visually to the strong
geometry of the existing library
designed by William Pereira.
The architect first proposed a
partially underground solution (p. 175
top). As built, the addition is entirely
underground (p. 175 bottom). Its
faceted glass walls, like transparent
fault lines in the rock, accentuate the
connection to the deep canyons in
the area. The "light canyons" are
planted with indigenous chaparral
mixed with cultivated ground cover
and plants. The underground areas
are given daylight on both floors
through skylights. These light portals
will be the addition's only
manifestation above ground at night.

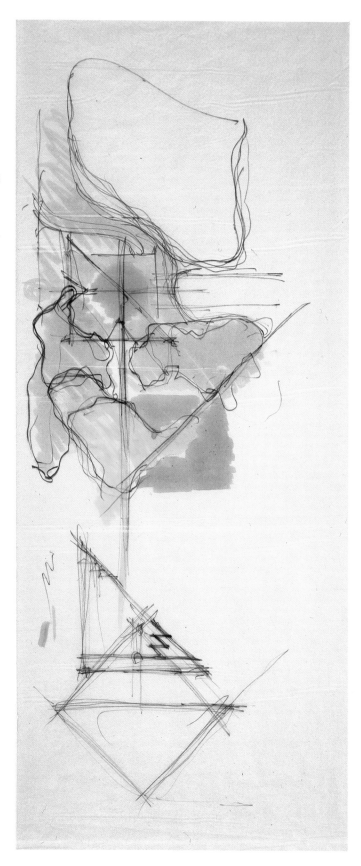

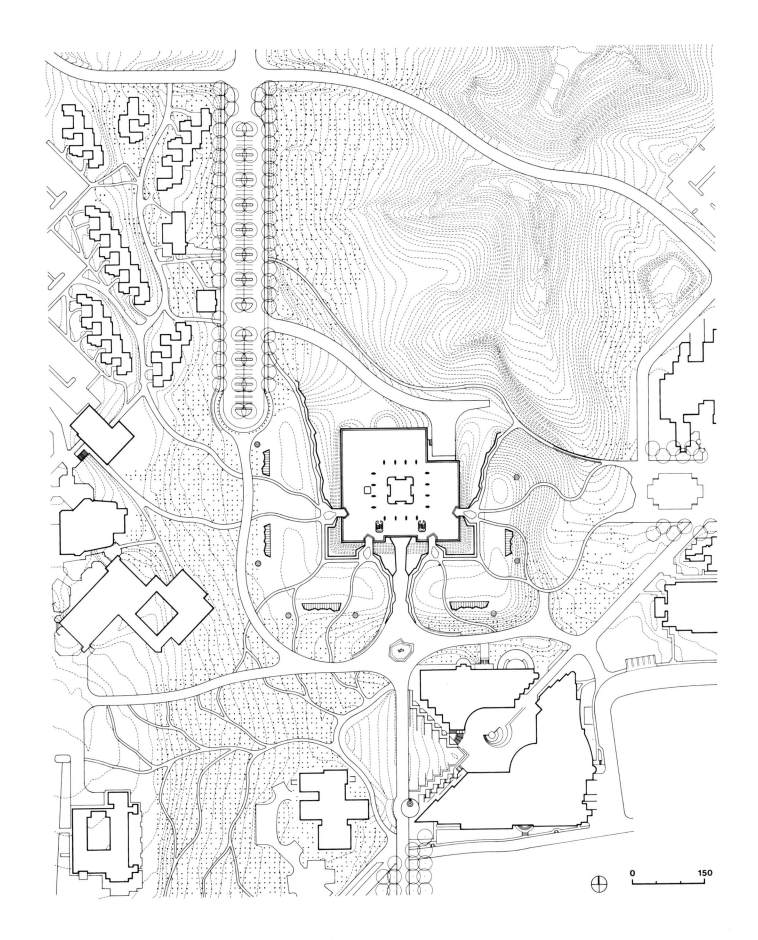

0   150

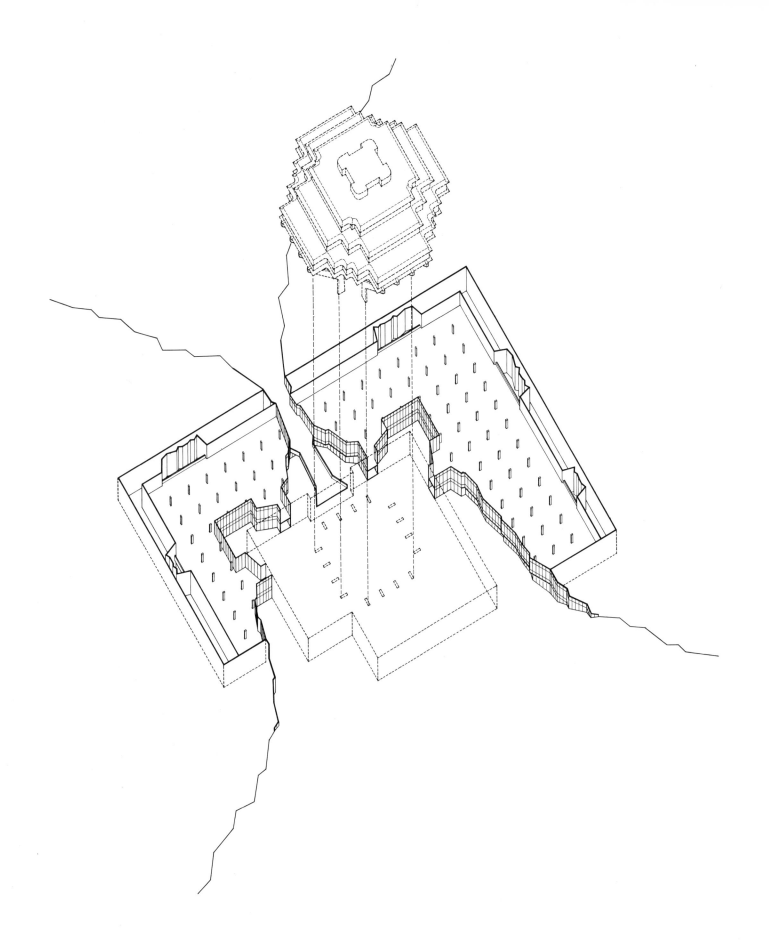

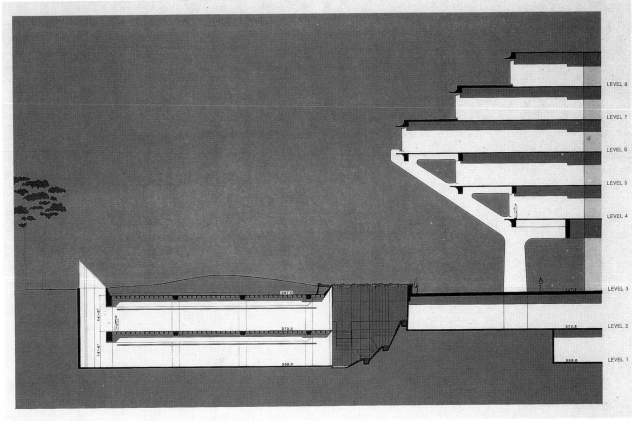

LEVEL 8

LEVEL 7

LEVEL 6

LEVEL 5

LEVEL 4

LEVEL 3

LEVEL 2

LEVEL 1

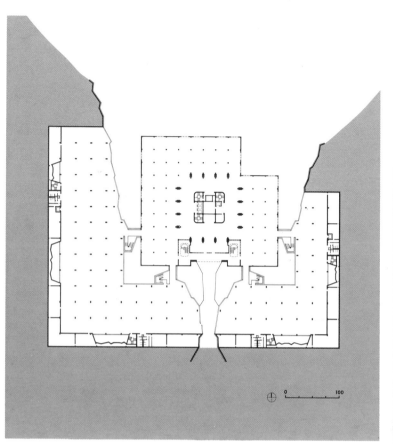

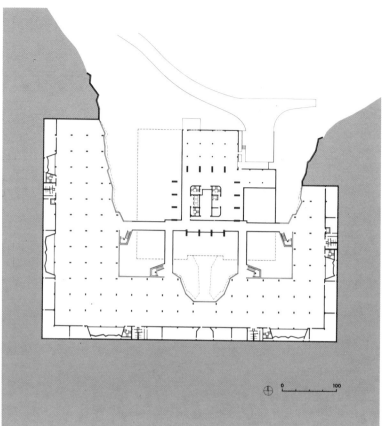

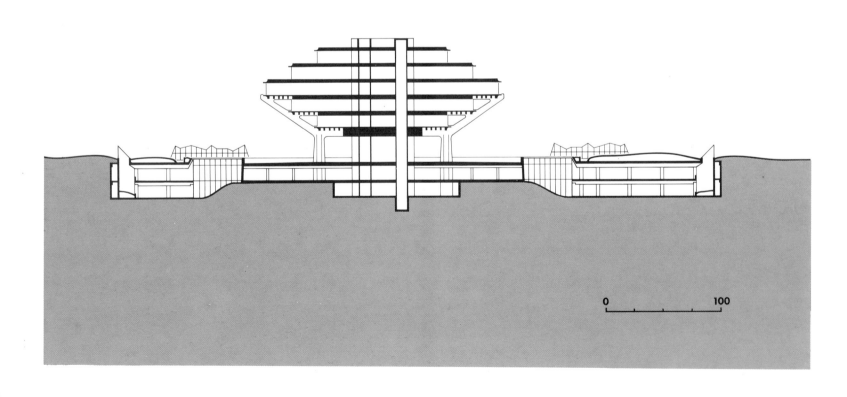

Domino's Farms Tower

Ann Arbor, Michigan, 1987
(in progress)

The architect's focus was the dynamic interaction between this tower and the landscape in a rural setting that presented none of the restrictions of an urban site. The structure is a cantilever, a 15-degree incline off the vertical, generating visual and emotional tension between building and ground plane. Birkerts imagines kinetic forces flowing from the heart of the building to the center of the earth.

The grid on the exterior glass skin graphically expresses the horizontal, the vertical and the 15-degree cantilever. The flow of color suggest sky, sun, water and vegetation above the green ground base.

Both architect and client sought an expressive building that would be a memorable symbol, but they wanted it for different reasons. Birkerts wanted a building that would evoke an emotional response. He wanted to "free the building from the vertical," to "surpass the traditional role of functional accommodation, visual complacency and the general attitudes of generic high-rise structures." The client wanted to be seen and remembered from the expressway.

The photograph on p. 182 shows the architect with a model at 1:10 scale on the site of the future building.

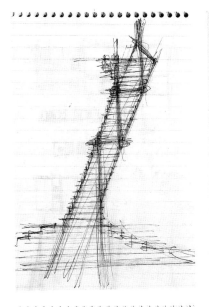

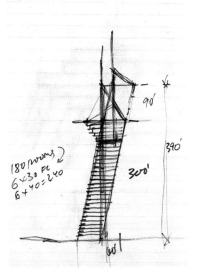

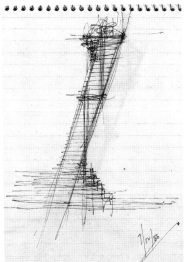

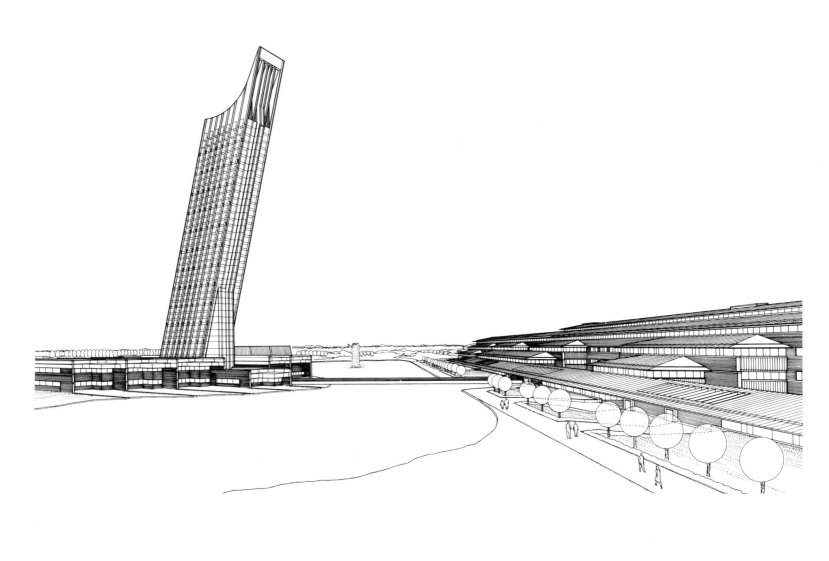

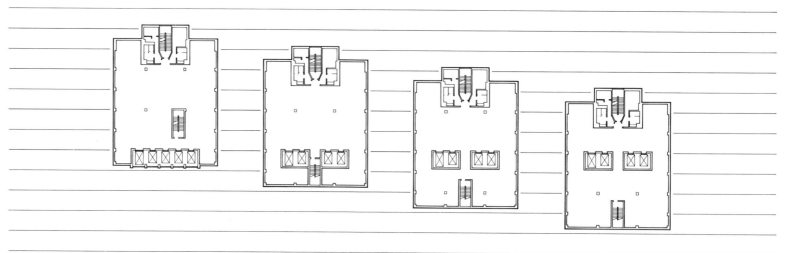

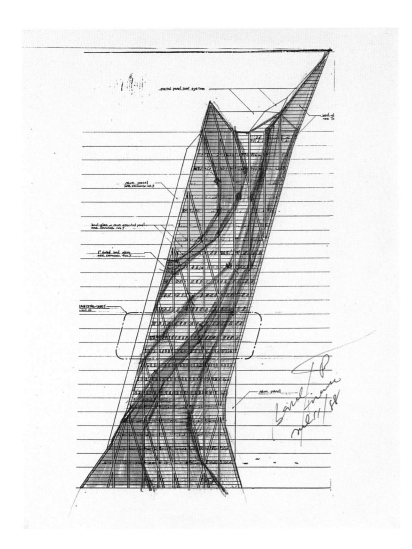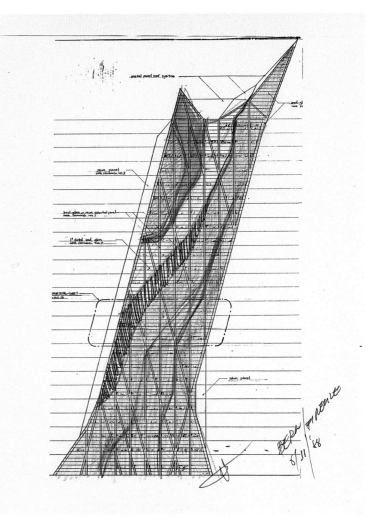

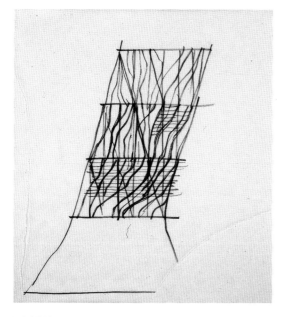

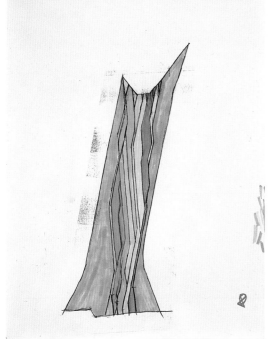

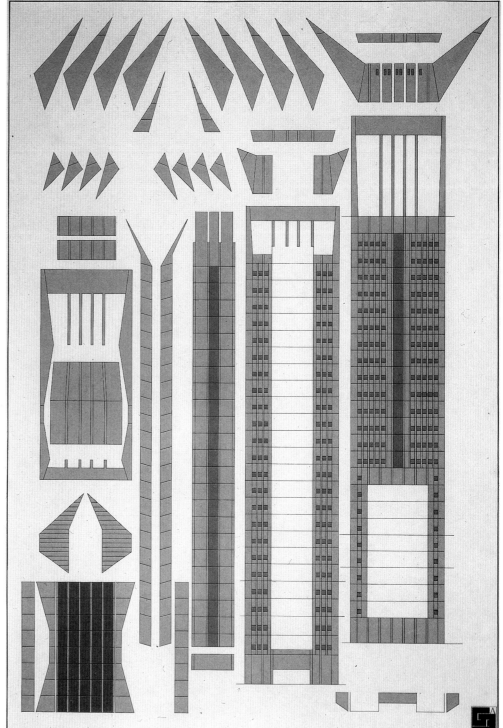

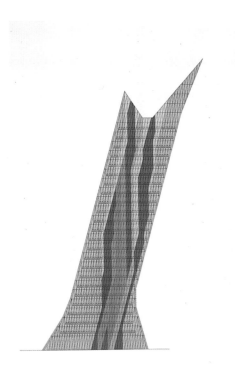

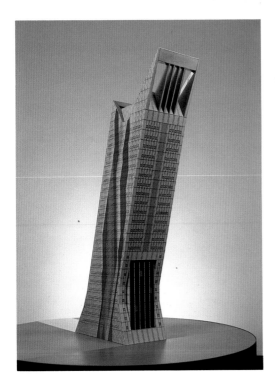

181

Papal Altar and Furniture, Pontiac Silverdome

Pontiac, Michigan, 1987 (1987)

A papal mass was held in the Pontiac Silverdome stadium during Pope John Paul II's visit to America. The furniture for John Paul II's mass (pp. 183-185) extended the design concept for the altar. The papal throne, a sculpture symbolizing organic growth, took the shape of a cupped hand that sheltered and accommodated the Holy Father. All the furniture was over-scaled because of the enormous size of the stadium.

Cardinal's chairs and the Acolytes' benches were designed in a vocabulary similar to that of the papal throne. The main altar was cherry wood. Its organic form reached from the platform to support the top, which held the liturgical pieces used in the service. The bases of the candle holders continued the theme. The metal processional cross was a direct representation of the plan of the papal mass platform.

The liturgical space designed for the observance had to assert its presence in the enormous Detroit Lions' football stadium.

Natural forms and organic material were used in the altar base. Wooden platforms and walkways accommodated circulation and seating. Materials native to the region – earth, water, wood, plants and stone – were brought into the stadium. Earth was mounded and covered with plants and flowers. All was encircled by a ring of water.

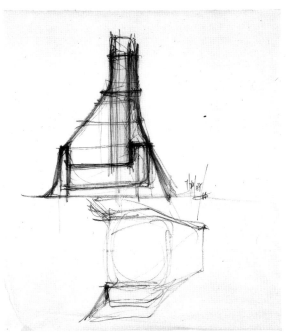

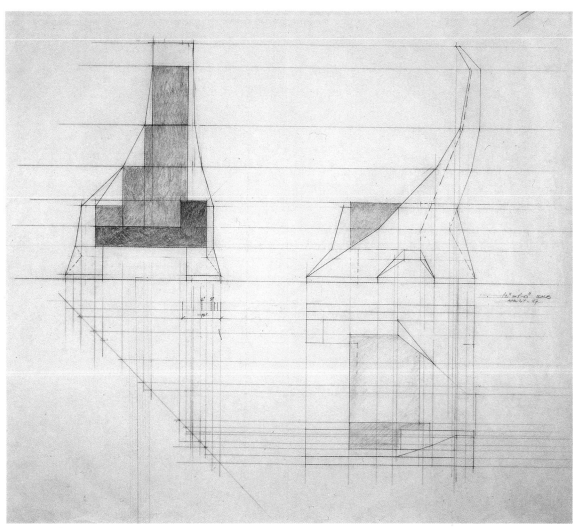

183

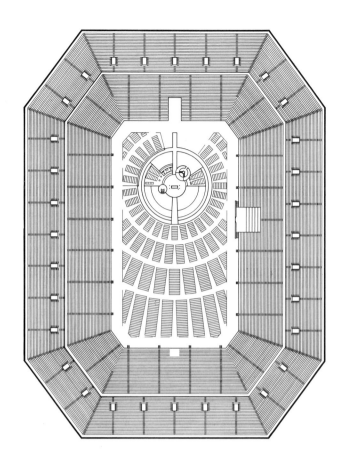

Honors College Building
Western Michigan University,
Kalamazoo, Michigan, 1987 (project)

The building synthesizes the
university's eccentric master plan
and the programmatic demand that
space in the new building be
arranged around a central reading
room.

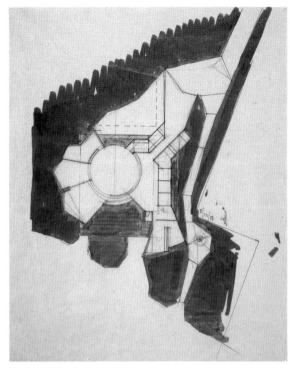

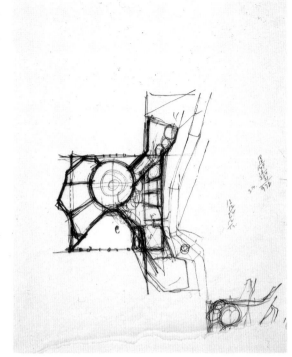

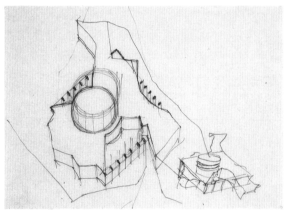

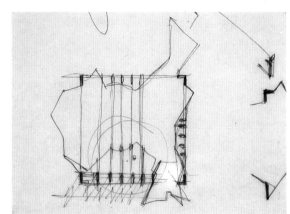

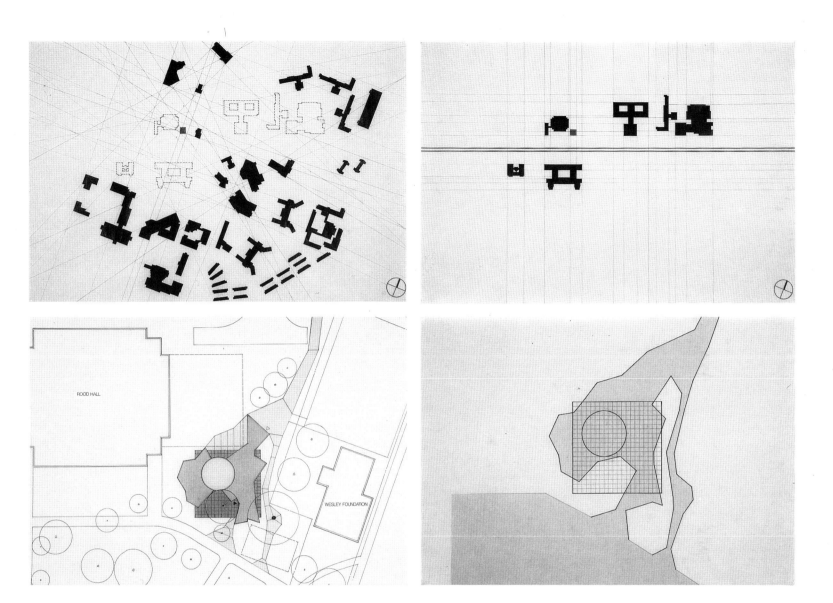

SITE PLAN

HONORS COLLEGE CENTER
WESTERN MICHIGAN UNIVERSITY

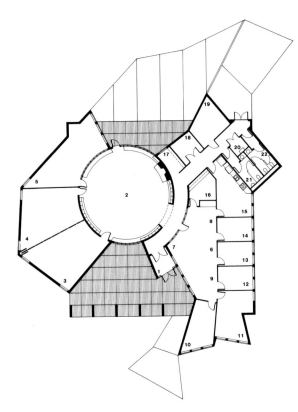

PLAN KEY

1. Vestibule
2. Honors Lounge
3. Seminar Room
4. Seminar Room
5. Library/Study Room
6. Receptionist/Secretary
7. Reception/Waiting
8. Office/Secretary
9. Administrative Secretary
10. Director's Office
11. Conference Room
12. Assistant Director's Office
13. Assistant Director's Office
14. Academic Advisor's Office
15. Kitchen/Workroom
16. Office Supply/Files
17. Coat Room
18. Storage Room
19. Mechanical/Electrical/ Telecommunications
20. Janitor's Closet
21. Men's Restroom
22. Women's Restroom

HONORS COLLEGE CENTER
WESTERN MICHIGAN UNIVERSITY
FLOOR PLAN

Novoli Multi-Use Center

Florence, Italy, 1988 (in progress)

When FIAT closed its manufacturing operation, a 70-acre tear was left in the fabric of Florence. Instead of using one designer, FIAT brought in a team of 14. San Francisco landscape architect and workshop specialist Lawrence Halprin directed the exercise in collective creativity that produced the master plan.

The existing urban fabric will reach into the development from all four sides. The nerve center fo the new project will be a public park at the center. Commercial, residential and office space extends from the park.

Architects Cappai & Mainardis, Roberto Gabetti, Aimaro Isola, Luigi Pellegrin, Leonardo Ricci, Richard Rogers, Aldo Loris Rossi and Birkerts are working on individual buildings in the development. Ralph Erskine participated in the design workshop and Bruno Zevi was a consultant to the city of Florence.

Birkerts' section of the project is an 865,000-square-foot mixed-use structure that includes office, commercial and residential space with three levels of parking that extend over the entire site, two levels below grade and one above.

Stairs and escalators are located in parking level light courts that bring daylight and visual awareness of the above-ground spaces to the parking levels.

The commercial level, on a platform above the street level parking and the park, is connected to the surrounding community by cascading stairs and landscaped terraces. The scale and urban texture of historic Florence are recaptured in the new building's clustered masses, varying heights and interconnecting pedestrian pathways.

Deliveries are made from the parking level below. There is no vehicular traffic at the commercial level. The side facing the park is lined with retail space devoted to service and recreational merchandise.

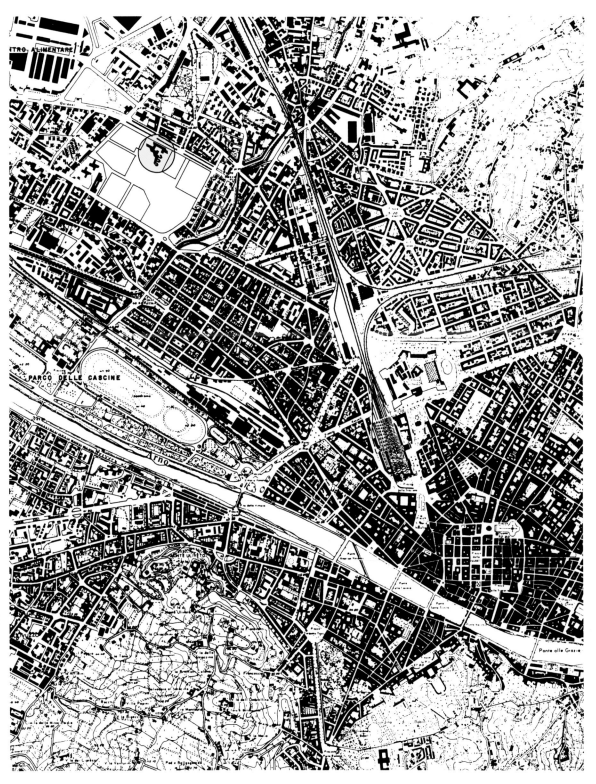

The commercial zone can extend vertically into the mezzanine and, in combination with the parking level commercial space, creates a three-level concept.

The office space can be reached directly from the parking levels, as well as from the commercial level through main lobbies. The office complex ranges from three to six floors, and can be divided horizontally or vertically, depending on tenant need. The space is serviced by the utility towers, stairs and elevators. Tenants requiring large or small spaces can be accommodated by this arrangement. The residential complex is composed of three six-story buildings. There are only three apartments per floor, and their segmented form allows for generous daylight and views from every room. Each building has its own roof garden and swimming pool.

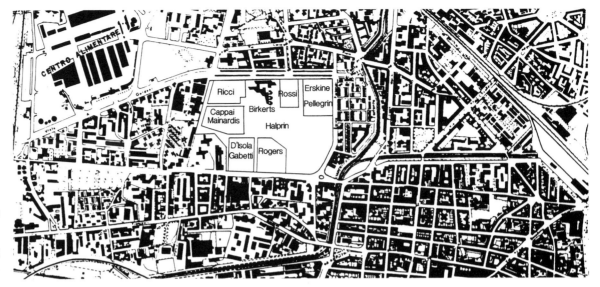

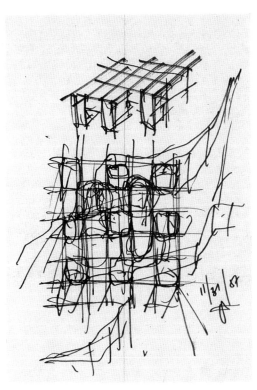

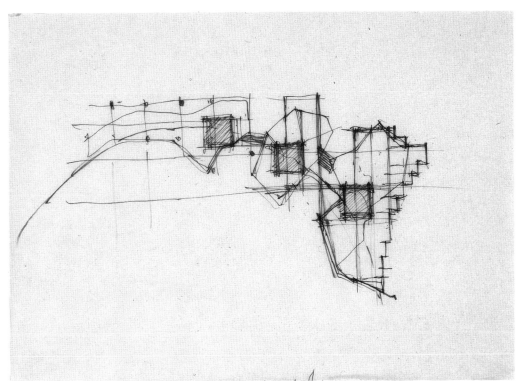

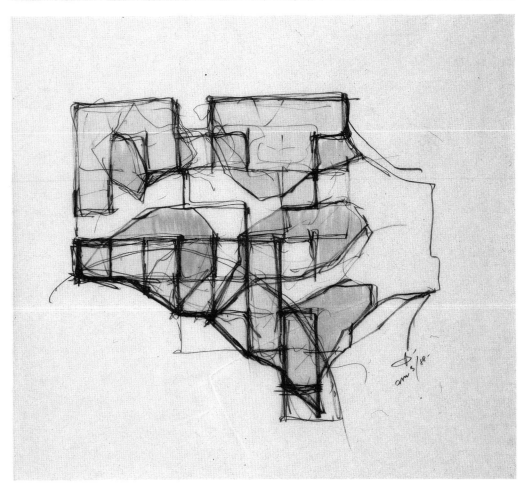

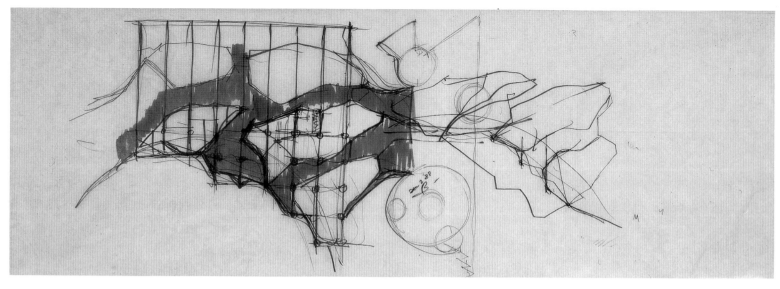

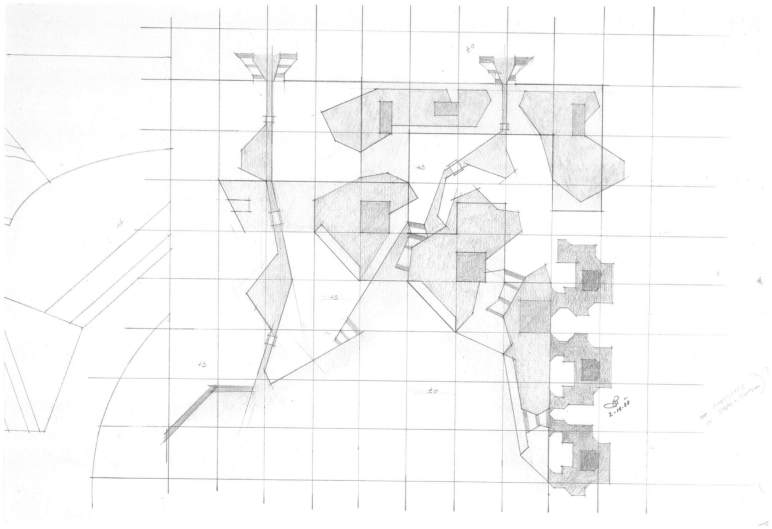

192

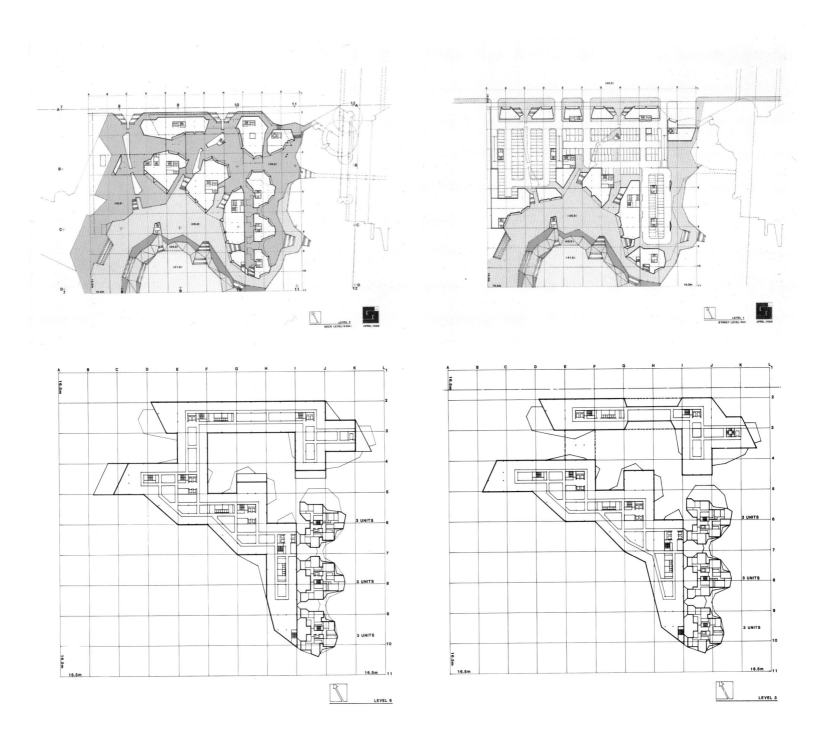

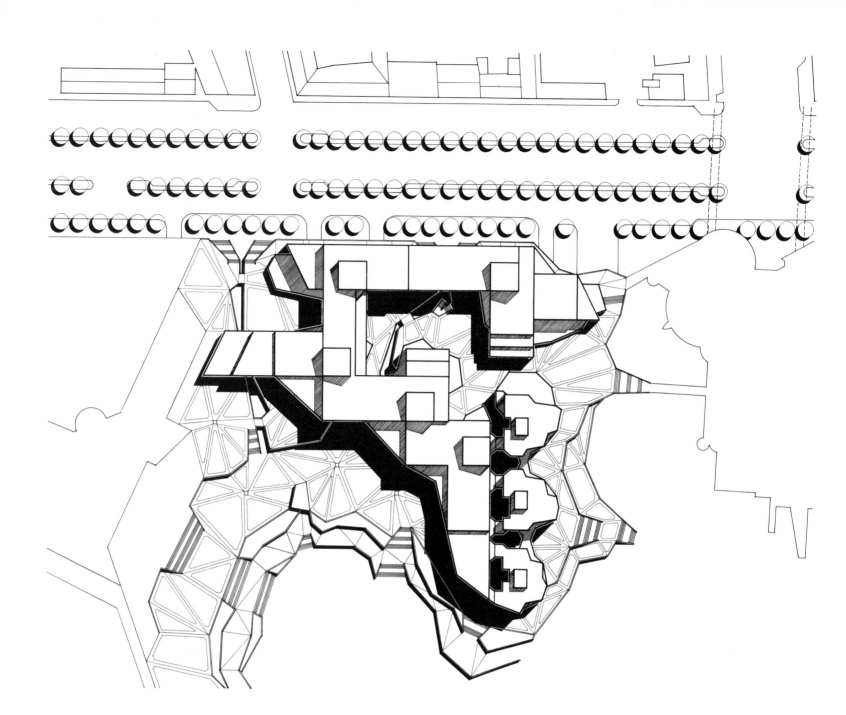

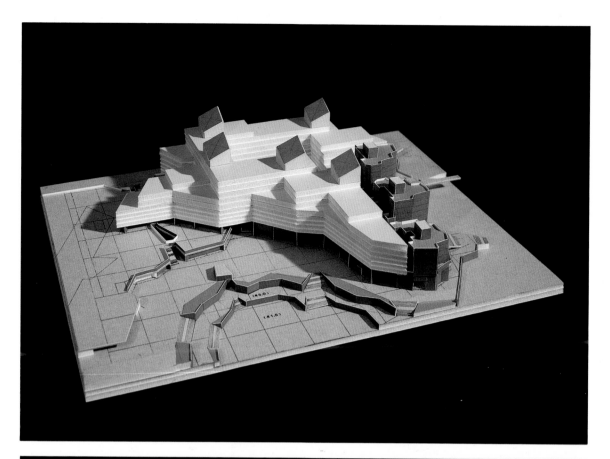

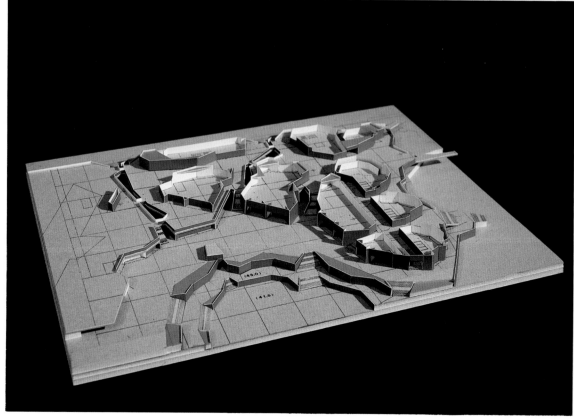

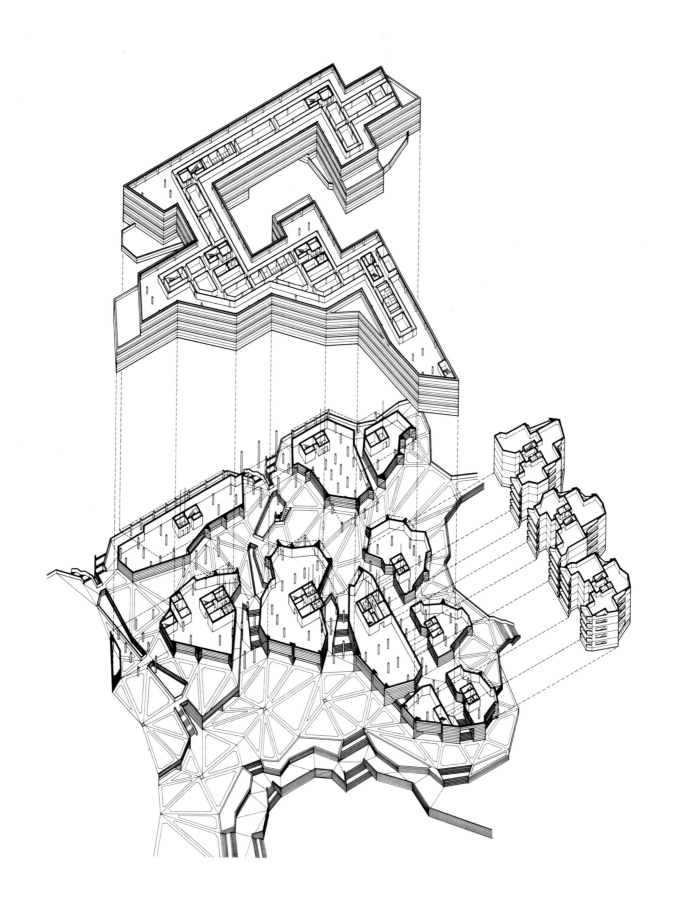

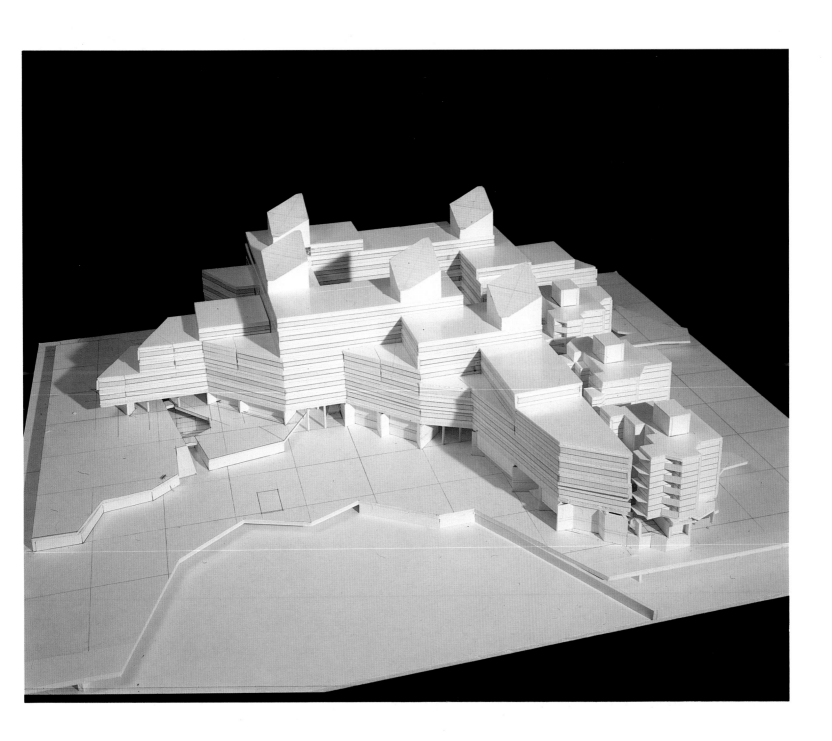

Michigan State Capitol Building Expansion Master Plan

Lansing, Michigan, 1987 (1987)

The Michigan state capitol, designed by Elija Myers and constructed between 1871 and 1878, was the first to emulate the scale and design of the U.S. Capitol in Washington, D.C. Many of Myers's details have been altered over the decades, but the structure is essentially intact. Proposed is a 400,000-square-foot, three-story subterranean office addition. It is designed as an ellipse that surrounds the capitol with expansive light wells that allow views to the capitol from all offices and public areas. The addition will house legislators, staff and fiscal agencies. Parking for 300-600 vehicles is also underground in a connected garage.

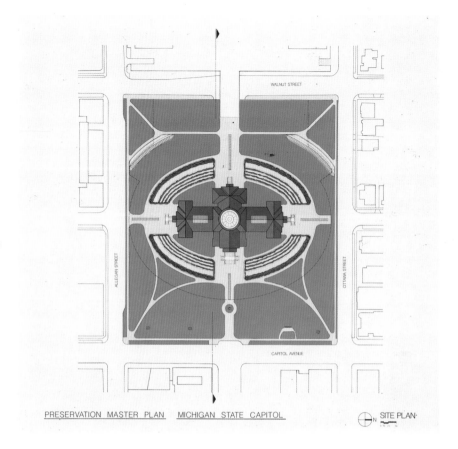

PRESERVATION MASTER PLAN   MICHIGAN STATE CAPITOL   N   SITE PLAN

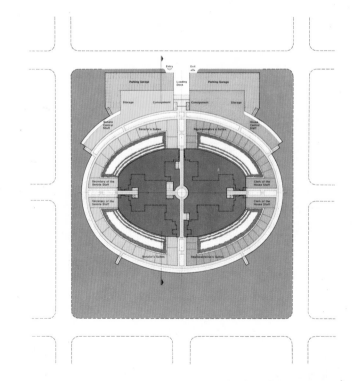

PRESERVATION MASTER PLAN   MICHIGAN STATE CAPITOL   N   LEVEL -1 PLAN

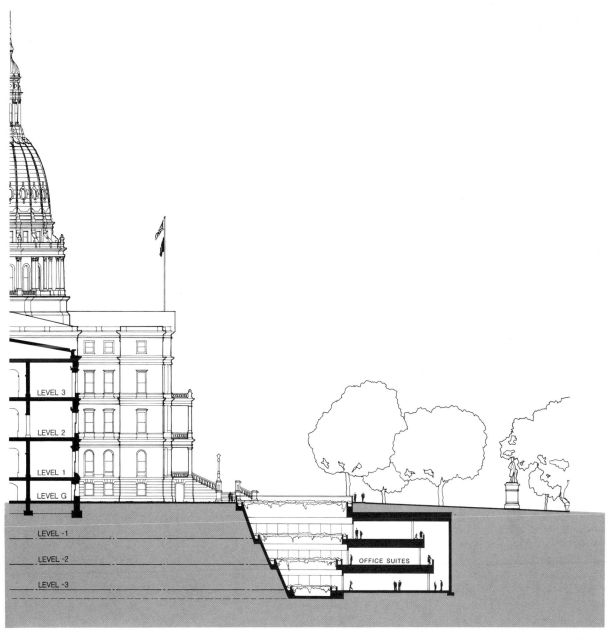

LEVEL 3

LEVEL 2

LEVEL 1

LEVEL G

LEVEL -1

LEVEL -2

OFFICE SUITES

LEVEL -3

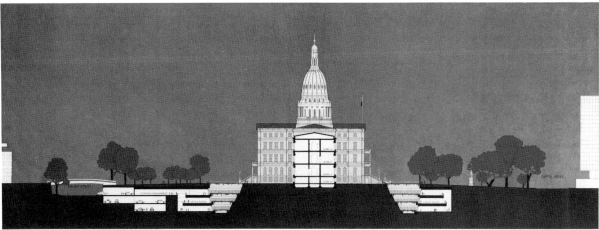

A SUGGESTED NEW CAPITOL GROUP
LANSING
MICHIGAN

HARLAND BARTHOLOMEW
CITY PLAN ENGINEER
SAINT LOUIS
1922

Ohio State University Law Building Addition

Columbus, Ohio, 1988 (in progress)

This is the third addition to the Ohio State law school, designed to unify the two existing sections and to create an identity for the new whole. The school is located on the southeast corner of the expansive urban university campus. The new building's role is to act as an introduction to the larger campus. The form recognizes this with its configuration: it literally points toward the center of the campus.

The configuration of the two exterior walls also provides the point of entry for the building. The limestone and bronze exterior responds to the prevailing campus vernacular and to the law school's existing structures. The elongated exterior walls allow more opportunity to bring daylight inside. The pattern of the punctured windows was determined by the amount of light required in certain areas.

A proposed colonnade would screen the incompatible facades of the existiing buildings. This element will also bring a unified image to the school.

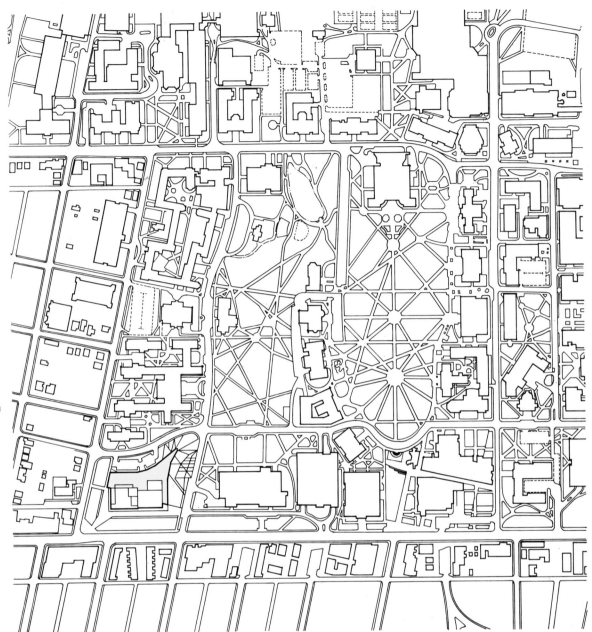

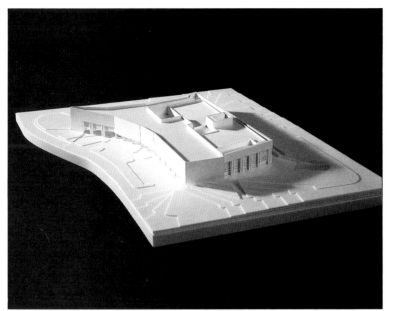

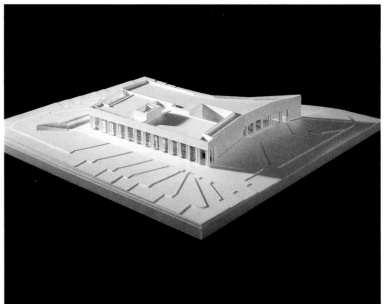

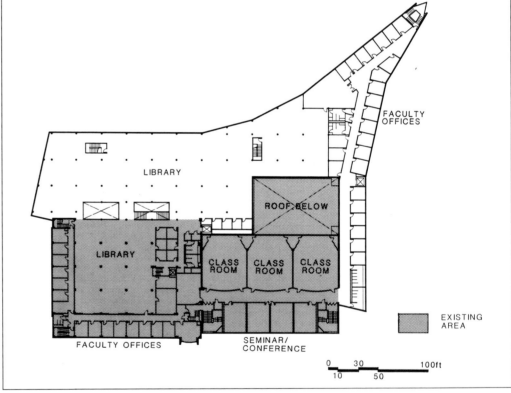

FACULTY OFFICES

LIBRARY

ROOF BELOW

LIBRARY

CLASS ROOM

CLASS ROOM

CLASS ROOM

EXISTING AREA

FACULTY OFFICES

SEMINAR/ CONFERENCE

0   30   100ft
10   50

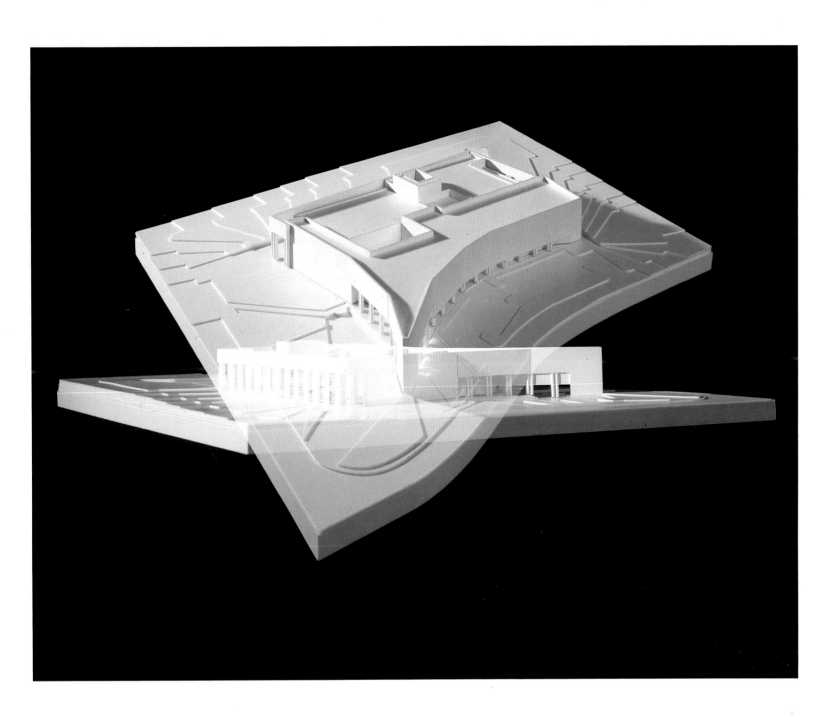

Marge Monaghan House

Drummond Island, Michigan, 1989
(in progress)

The architectural form of this vacation
house on an island in Lake Huron
draws on the natural shapes, forms
and forces in the landscape. The site
is to be left untouched except for the
necessary intrusion of the process of
building.

The wood frame structure is
sheathed in copper and is expected
to assume a greenish-brown patina
over the years. On the interior, the
spaces are completely lined with
wood of different types, textures and
finishes.

The parents' quarters and the
common social spaces are on the
ground floor. The second floor
accommodates four daughters and
their families.

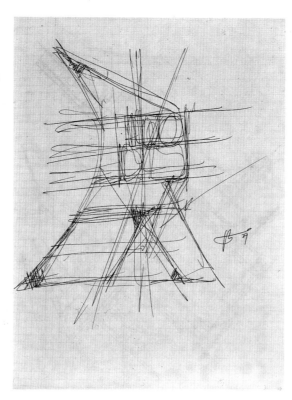

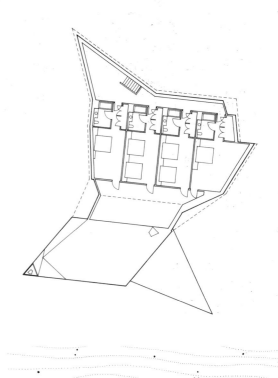

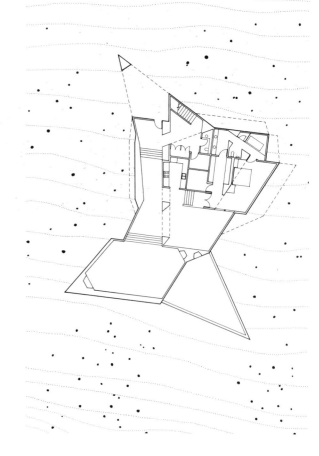

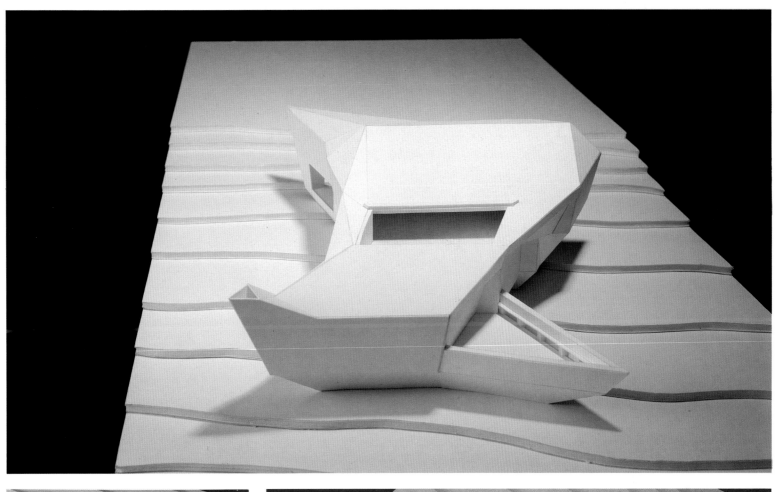
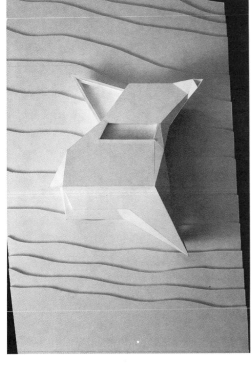
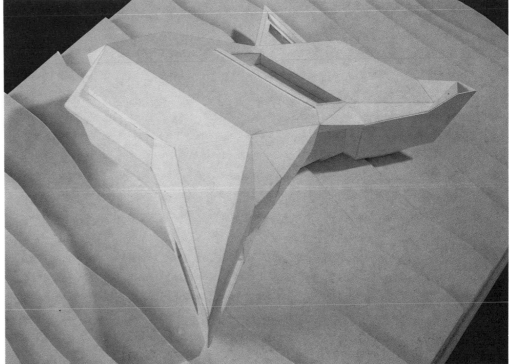

"The Next One..."
1989

This office building, shown in the
early concept stage, is tucked into a
mountainside. Its form responds to
the geology underneath and
expresses the imagery of the nearby
rock formations.

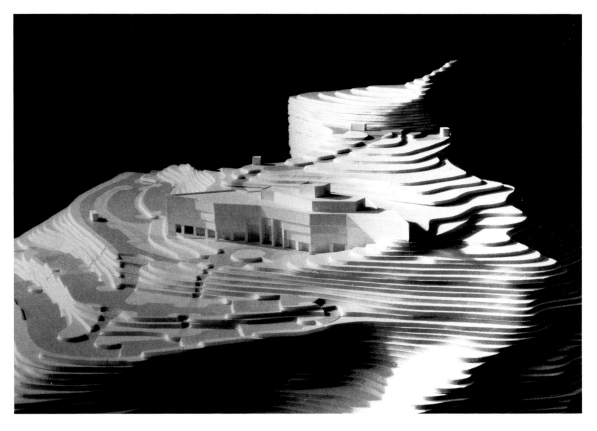

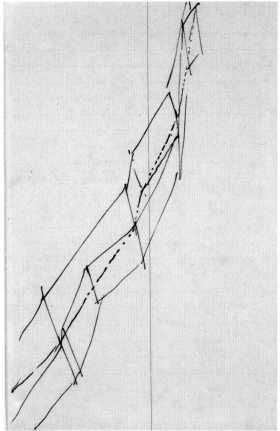

Biographical Data
Complete List of Projects
Selected Bibliography
Credits

Biographical Data

1925
Born in Riga, Latvia

1945
Enters Technische Hochschule, Stuttgart, Germany

1949
Receives Diplomingenieur-Architekt degree from Technische Hochschule, Stuttgart, Germany
Arrives in United States

1950
Works in the office of Perkins and Will, Chicago

1951
Joins the office of Eero Saarinen in Bloomfield Hills, Michigan

1954
Named Young Designer of the Year, Akron Institute of Art

1955
First Prize, International Furniture Competition, Cantù, Italy

1956
Joins the office of Minoru Yamasaki in Birmingham, Michigan

1959
Establishes own practice (Birkerts & Straub, Birmingham, Michigan)

1961
Assistant Professor of Architecture, University of Michigan

1962
Establishes Gunnar Birkerts and Associates, Birmingham, Michigan

1963
Associate Professor of Architecture, University of Michigan

1969
Professor of Architecture, University of Michigan

1970
Elected Fellow, American Institute of Architects

1971
Gold Medal in Architecture from Tau Sigma Delta
Honorary Fellow, Latvian Architects Association
Fellow, Graham Foundation

1975
Gold Medal from American Institute of Architects, Detroit

1976
Architect in Residence, American Academy in Rome

1980
Gold Medal, Michigan Society of Architects

1981
Arnold W. Brunner Memorial Prize in Architecture, The American Academy and Institute of Arts and Letters

1982
First Recipient of the Lawrence J. Plym Distinguished Professorship in Architecture at the University of Illinois

1984
First Recipient of the Thomas S. Monaghan
Architect-In-Residence
Professorship in Architecture at the University of Michigan

1986
Honored for Outstanding Achievement by the Association for the Advancement of Baltic Studies

1988
Michigan Arts Award, Arts Foundation of Michigan
"Domino's 30" Award, Top 30 Architects for 1988, Domino's Pizza Inc.

Complete List of Projects

Mequon House, 1957 (project)
Mequon, Wisconsin

Aluminum House, 1958 (project)
Virgin Islands

Cultural Center of Leopoldville, Competition, 1958 (project)
Leopoldville, Belgian Congo

Technical University Competition, 1959 (project)
Ankara, Turkey

Roosevelt Competition, Roosevelt Island, 1960 (project)
New York, New York

Schwartz Summer Residence, 1960 (1962)
Northville, Michigan

Troy Country Club - Bath House, 1960 (project)
Troy, Michigan

Cranbrook Country Club - Bath House, 1960 (project)
Bloomfield Hills, Michigan

Haley Funeral Home, 1960 (1961)
Southfield, Michigan

Albion Church, 1960 (project)
Albion, Michigan

Taubman Residence, 1960 (1962)
Southfield, Michigan

1300 Lafayette East Apartments, 1961 (1963)
Detroit, Michigan

Wrigley Supermarket, 1961 (project)
Detroit, Michigan

Big Value Supermarket, 1961 (project)
Detroit, Michigan

Honigman, Miller, Schwartz, Cohen, Law Offices, 1961 (1962)
Detroit, Michigan

Cleveland Apartment Competition
Towne Plaza Apartments, 1961 (project)
Cleveland, Ohio

Apartments, 1961 (project)
Lansing, Michigan

Kaufman Residence, 1962 (project)
Muskegon, Michigan

Ash-Stevens Research Laboratory, 1962 (1963)
Detroit, Michigan

Marathon Oil Office Building, 1962 (1964)
Detroit, Michigan

Lillibridge Elementary School Addition, 1962 (1963)
Detroit, Michigan

Peoples Federal Savings and Loan Bank, Branch Office, 1962 (1963)
Royal Oak, Michigan

University Reformed Church, 1963 (1964)
Ann Arbor, Michigan

International Village, 1964 (project)
Detroit, Michigan

Bald Mountain Recreation Facility, 1964 (1969)
Pontiac, Michigan

Detroit Institute of Arts – South Wing Addition, 1964 (1964)
Detroit, Michigan

Elmwood Housing, 1964 (project)
Detroit, Michigan

Kaufman House Number 2, 1964 (1964)
Muskegon, Michigan

Fisher Administrative Center, University of Detroit, 1964 (1966)
Detroit, Michigan

Travis Residence, 1964 (1965)
Bloomfield Hills, Michigan

E.O.C. Kentucky, 1964 (study)
A City Hall with "Emergency Operation Center"
Wind City, Illinois

Freeman Residence, 1965 (1966)
Grand Rapids, Michigan

Lincoln Elementary School, 1965 (1967)
Columbus, Indiana

Lewis Furniture Store, 1965 (project)
Bloomfield Hills, Michigan

Livonia Public Library, 1965 (1967)
Livonia, Michigan

Al Green's Restaurant, 1965 (project)
Detroit, Michigan & Philadelphia, Pennsylvania

Lewis Residence, 1965 (1967)
Bloomfield Hills, Michigan

Tougaloo College Campus Master Plan, 1965 (project)
Tougaloo, Mississippi

Michigan Tech University – Dormitory, 1965 (1967)
Saulte Ste. Marie, Michigan

Michigan Tech University – Food Service Center, 1965 (1968)
Saulte Ste. Marie, Michigan

Grasis Residence, 1965 (1966)
Kansas City, Missouri

Bardha Beauty Salon, 1965 (1966)
Birmingham, Michigan

Massey Ferguson North American Operations Offices, 1966 (project)
Des Moines, Iowa

Glen Oaks Community College, 1966 (1971)
Centreville, Michigan

Corning Glass Company, Plant I Master Plan, 1966 (project)
Corning, New York

Tougaloo College Dormitories, 1966 (1972)
Tougaloo, Mississippi

Tougaloo College Library, 1966 (1972)
Tougaloo, Mississippi

(Complete List of Projects)

Church of St. Bede, 1966 (1969)
Southfield, Michigan

Morent Olive Baptist Church, 1967
(1970)
Detroit, Michigan

Vocational Technical Institute Campus
Master Plan, 1967 (project)
Carbondale, Illinois

Ford Pavilion of Hemisfair '68,
1967 (1968)
San Antonio, Texas

Amsterdam City Hall Competition,
1968 (project)
Amsterdam, Netherlands

Federal Reserve Bank of Minneapolis,
1968 (1973)
Minneapolis, Minnesota

Ford Rouge Office Building, 1968
(project)
Detroit, Michigan

Corning Public Library, First Proposal,
1969 (project)
Corning, New York

Corning Public Library, Final Proposal,
1969 (project)
Corning, New York

Columbus Commercial Strip Master
Plan, 1969 (study)
Columbus, Indiana

Metropolitan Federal Savings and Loan
Bank, 1969 (project)
Southfield, Michigan

IBM Corporate Computer Center,
1970 (1972)
Sterling Forest, New York

Contemporary Arts Museum, 1970
(1972)
Houston, Texas

Visitor Reception Center (scheme 1)
Ford Motor Company, 1971 (project)
Dearborn, Michigan

Dance Instructional Facility, 1971 (1976)
State University of New York, Purchase

Visitor Reception Center (scheme 2)
Ford Motor Company, 1972 (1975)
Dearborn, Michigan

3M Microfilm Modular Cabinetry,
1972 (1972)

Federal Reserve Bank of Helena,
1972 (project)
Helena, Montana

Outdoor Chapel, Latvian Center,
1972 (1972)
Garezers, Three Rivers, Michigan

Museum of Glass (I), 1972 (project)
Corning, New York

Washington Monument Visitor Center
Competition, 1972 (project)
Washington, D.C.

Municipal Fire Station, 1973 (1974)
Corning, New York

General Motors Transportation Studies:
Dual Mode System, 1973 (1974)

General Motors Transportation Studies:
GM Technical Center, 1973 (project)
Warren, Michigan

General Motors Transportation Studies:
Urban Loop, 1973 (project)
Detroit, Michigan

Foley Manufacturing Company Master
Plan, 1973 (project)
Minneapolis, Minnesota

GMC Test Facility Building and Track,
1974 (project)
Pueblo, Colorado

Calvary Baptist Church, 1974 (1977)
Detroit, Michigan

Detroit Bank & Trust Renovation,
1974 (1981)
Detroit, Michigan

University of Michigan Law School
Addition (I), 1974 (project)
Ann Arbor, Michigan

University of Michigan Law School
Addition (II), 1974 (1981)
Ann Arbor, Michigan

IBM Office Building, 1974 (1979)
Southfield, Michigan

First Citizens Bank, 1974 (1975)
Troy, Michigan

Subterranean Urban Systems Study,
1974 (study)
Graham Foundation Grant

U.S. Embassy Office Building,
1975 (project)
Helsinki, Finland

Steuben Glass/Algernon Asprey,
1975 (project)
London, England

Duluth Public Library, 1976 (1980)
Duluth, Minnesota

Museum of Glass (II), 1976 (1980)
Corning, New York

IBM Corporation/Renaissance Center
Interiors, 1977 (1978)
Detroit, Michigan

Holder-Birkerts Design Competition,
1977 (project)

Federated Department Stores Office
Building, 1977 (project)
Cincinnati, Ohio

AMSTORE/Architectural and Interior
Remodeling, 1978 (project)
Grand Rapids, Michigan

Unity of the Infinite Presence,
1978 (project)
Warren, Michigan

Chrysler Corporation Computer Facility,
1978 (project)
Highland Park, Michigan

Corning Glass Works/Orientation
Theatre, 1978 (project)
Corning, New York

Chrysler Corporation Master Plan,
1978 (project)
Highland Park and Detroit, Michigan

Housing Competition, 1979 (project)
Amman, Jordan

Latvian Canadian Cultural Centre,
1979 (1980)
Master Plan and Design (Toronto)

J.A. Citrin Sons Company Office
Building, 1979 (project)
Bingham Farms, Michigan

AMSTORE, 1979 (1980)
Greenville, South Carolina

Broad Corporation Corporate Offices,
1979 (1982)
Allen Park, Michigan

Muiznieks Residence, 1979 (project)
Kalamazoo, Michigan

University of Iowa College of Law
Building, 1979 (1986)
Iowa City, Iowa

Cathedral of the Most Blessed
Sacrament Renovation, 1980 (project)
Detroit, Michigan

Ferguson Residence, 1980 (1983)
Kalamazoo, Michigan

Cornell University Uris Library Addition,
1980 (1982)
Ithaca, New York

Baldwin Public Library Addition,
1980 (1983)
Birmingham, Michigan

Chapel and Educational Facility, U.S.
Army, 1980 (1983)
Camp Wildflecken, Germany

St. Peter's Lutheran Church, 1980
(1988)
Columbus, Indiana

University of Nebraska, Wick Alumni
Center Competition, 1981 (project)
Lincoln, Nebraska

Anchorage Library Competition,
1981 (project)
Anchorage, Alaska

Corning Glass Works Fifth Avenue
Offices, 1981 (project)
New York, New York

State of Wisconsin Office Building,
1981 (1983)
Green Bay, Wisconsin

Woodbranch Energy Plaza,
1982 (project)
Houston, Texas

University of Michigan Law Library Rare
Book Display, 1982 (project)
Ann Arbor, Michigan

Chrysler Corporation Executive Offices,
1982 (project)
Highland Park, Michigan

University of Michigan, Knoxville
Charrette, 1982 (project)
Knoxville, Tennessee

ParkCenter, 1983 (project)
Houston, Texas

IBM Southfield Centre Earth Station,
1983 (1984)
Southfield, Michigan

AMSTORE Warehouse Addition,
1983 (1984)
Liberty, South Carolina

Holtzman & Silverman Office Building,
1983 (1989)
Southfield, Michigan

Lewis Residence, 1983 (1984)
Bloomfield Hills, Michigan

Carodan Office Building, 1983 (project)
Toledo, Ohio

Domino's Farms Master Plan,
1984 (1984)
Ann Arbor, Michigan

Domino's Pizza, Inc. Headquarters,
1984 (in progress)
Ann Arbor, Michigan

IBM Beecher Road Facility, 1984 (1985)
Flint, Michigan

Comerica Personal Banking Center,
1984 (1984)
Detroit, Michigan

Minnesota Judicial Building
Competition, 1984 (project)
St. Paul, Minnesota

Minnesota History Center Competition,
1984 (project)
St. Paul, Minnesota

Bardha Residence, 1984 (1989)
Birmingham, Michigan

Law School Feasibility Study, 1985
(1985)
Duke University, Durham, North Carolina

Domino's Pizza, Inc., Special Designs,
1985 (1986)
Ann Arbor, Michigan

University of Michigan Sports Services
Building, 1985 (in progress)
Ann Arbor, Michigan

Prototypical School Competition,
1986 (project)
Las Vegas, Nevada

Conservatory of Music Library Addition,
1986 (1988)
Oberlin, Ohio

Domino's Pizza, Inc. Prototypical
Franchise Building, 1986 (1988)
Jackson, Michigan

Residence, 1986 (project)
San Francisco, California

Library, University of Michigan – Flint,
1986 (in progress)

Selected Bibliography

Books

American Institute of Architects, Detroit Chapter. *Detroit Architecture AIA Guide.* 2d ed., rev. Edited by Martin C.P. McElory. Detroit: Wayne State University Press, 1980, pp. 63, 84, 125, 136, 145, 151, 158, 194, 214, 239, 254.

Birkerts, Gunnar. *Gunnar Birkerts: Buildings, Projects and Thoughts, 1960-1985.* Edited by Sven Peter Birkerts. Ann Arbor: University of Michigan, College of Architecture and Urban Planning, 1985.

Buildings for the Arts. New York: McGraw-Hill, 1978, pp. 42, 43, 50, 51.

Bugbee, Gordon P. Introduction to *Domino's Mansion: Thomas Monaghan, Gunnar Birkerts, and the Spirit of Frank Lloyd Wright,* by Vincent Scully. Carbondale: Southern Illinois University Press, 1988.

Carmody, John, and Sterling, Raymond. *Underground Building Design.* New York: Van Nostrand Reinhold Co., 1983, pp. 14, 15, 52, 53, 68-75.

Caudill, William W., et al. *Architecture & You: How to Experience and Enjoy Buildings.* New York: Whitney Library of Design, 1978, pp. 32, 54, 100, 159.

Dean, Andrea Oppenheimer. *Bruno Zevi on Modern Architecture.* New York: Rizzoli, 1983, p. 78.

Emanuel, Muriel. *Contemporary Architects.* New York: St. Martin's, 1980, pp. 95-96.

Ferry, W. Hawkins. *The Buildings of Detroit.* Detroit: Wayne State University Press, 1968, pp. 376, 381, 388, 393.

Heyne, Pamela. *Today's Architectural Mirror: Interiors, Buildings and Solar Designs.* New York: Van Nostrand Reinhold, 1982, pp. 29, 66, 70, 71, 145-147.

Heyer, Paul. *Architects on Architecture.* New York: Walker & Co., 1978, p. 406.

Ikonnikov, A.V. *Arkhitektura SSHA.* Moscow: Iskusstvo, 1979, pp. 138, 139.

Jencks, Charles. *Architecture Today.* New York: Abrams, 1982, pp. 58, 60, 304.

Kepes, Gyorgy. *Arts of the Environment.* Mississippi: Tougaloo College, 1972, pp. 146-147.

Kidder Smith, G.E. *A Pictorial History of Architecture in America.* New York: American Heritage, 1976, pp. 516, 518-519.

Kulski, Julian Eugene. *Architecture in a Revolutionary Era.* Nashville, Tenn.: Aurora, 1971.

Kultermann, Udo. *New Architecture in the World.* Boulder, Colorado: Westview Press, 1976.

Marlin, William. "The Longest Baltic Current," *GA Architect 2: Gunnar Birkerts and Associates.* Tokyo: A.D.A. EDITA, 1982.

McCoy, Esther. *GA 31: IBM Information Center and Federal Reserve Bank.* Tokyo: A.D.A. EDITA, 1974.

Morgan, Ann L., and Naylor, Colin. *Contemporary Architects.* 2d rev. ed. Chicago: St. James Press, 1987, pp. 99, 100.

Stephens, John H. *Towers, Bridges and Other Structures.* New York: Guinness Books, 1978, p. 93.

Stimpson, Miriam F. *A Field Guide to Landmarks of Modern Architecture in the United States.* Englewood Cliffs, N.J.: Prentice Hall, 1985, pp. 196, 202, 203, 204, 209, 216, 221, 264, 281, 373.

Turner, Paul Venable. *Campus: An American Planning Tradition.* Cambridge, Mass.: MIT Press, 1984, pp. 267, 271, 272.

Journals and Periodicals

Living, November 1954: "Young Designer of 1954," p. 134.

Mobilia (Denmark), April 1956: vol. 22, no. 4, "Gunnar Birkerts: Cantù Competition," pp. 38, 39.

Progressive Architecture, January 1957: Design Awards Program, Vacation House, Mequon, Wisconsin, pp. 128, 129, 144, 145.

Progressive Architecture, January 1959: Design Awards Program, Prefabricated Aluminum House, p. 142.

Progressive Architecture, January 1961: Eighth Annual Design Awards, Swimming Club, Troy, Michigan, pp. 130, 131.

Architectural Record, Mid-May 1961: Record Houses of 1961 (Residence, Northville, Michigan), pp. 120-122.

Progressive Architecture, August 1961: "Detroit's New Generation," pp. 106-113.

Progressive Architecture, December 1961: "Form in Churches" (University Reformed Church, Ann Arbor, Michigan), pp. 119-121.

Art in America, 1962, no. 1: "New Talent USA," p. 52.

Progressive Architecture, June 1962: "Shadows on the Wall" (Haley Funeral Home, Southfield, Michigan), pp. 102-107.

Interiors, August 1962: "Palladian Symmetry for the Twentieth Century" (Residence, Northville, Michigan), pp. 86-89.

Casabella (Italy), November 1962, no. 269: University Reformed Church, Haley Funeral Home.

Architectural Record, January 1963: "Redevelopment Combines Highrise and Townhouses" (Lafayette Apartments), pp. 144-146.

Progressive Architecture, March 1963: "Cubist Corners" (Federal Savings and Loan Bank), pp. 130-133.

Architectural Forum, November 1963: "Urban Schools" (Lillibridge Elementary School, Detroit, Michigan).

Casabella (Italy), November 1983, no. 281: "Philologia della Architettura Americana" (Federal Savings and Loan Bank, Lillibridge Elementary School), p. 38.

Zodiac 13 (Italy), 1963: "Young Architects in the US," pp. 164-197.

Deutsche Bauzeitschrift (Germany), 1964, no. 6: "Summer House near Detroit" (Residence, Northville, Michigan), pp. 885-886.

Architectural Record, August 1964: "Step Terne Roofs Shelter Funeral Chapels" (Haley Funeral Home), p. 56.

Progressive Architecture, September 1964: "A Search for Architectural Principles–Some Thoughts and Works of Gunnar Birkerts," pp. 172-191.

L'Architettura (Italy), January 1965, no. 111: Lillibridge Elementary School, University Reformed Church, pp. 618, 619.

Progressive Architecture, April 1965: "Urban University Gets Image Making Entrance" (Fisher Administrative Center, University of Detroit), pp. 224-227.

L'Architecture d'Aujord'hui (France), September 1965: "USA '65" (University Reformed Church), pp. 70-71.

Architectural Forum, December 1965: "Columbus, Indiana" (Lincoln Elementary School), p. 48.

Architectural Forum, April 1966: "How to Grow a Campus" (Tougaloo College, Mississippi), pp. 56-61.

Progressive Architecture, April 1966: "Matriculation Matrix" (Tougaloo College, Mississippi), pp. 211-213.

Werk (Switzerland), July 1966: Tougaloo College, Mississippi, pp. 174-175.

Architectural Record, August 1966: "Newest Projects of Gunnar Birkerts," pp. 93-106.

Architectural Review (England), October 1966, vol. 140, no. 836: "The Expanding Campus" (Tougaloo College, Mississippi), p. 233.

Architectural Record, July 1967: "Fisher Administrative Center," University of Detroit, pp. 109-113.

(Selected Bibliography)

Nation's Schools, October 1967, vol. 80, no. 4: "The Nation's School of the Month" (Lincoln Elementary School, Columbus, Indiana), pp. 101-103.

Architectural Forum, November 1967: "The School That Will Vanish" (Lincoln Elementary School), pp. 48-53.

Life, November 17, 1967: "An Inspired Renaissance in Indiana" (Lincoln Elementary School), pp. 74-84.

Architectural Record, Mid-May 1968: Record Houses of 1968, "Atrium House, Grand Rapids, Michigan," pp. 64-67.

Progressive Architecture, August 1968: "Corners," pp. 96-98.

Interior Design (England), September 1968: Pavilion, San Antonio, Texas, p. 63.

Architectural Record, October 1968: "Three Colleges by Gunnar Birkerts," pp. 129-144.

College and University Business, December 1968: "College Building of the Month" (Fisher Administration Building, University of Detroit), pp. 48-50.

Lotus 4 (Italy), 1967-1968: Tougaloo College, Mississippi and Fisher Administrative Building, University of Detroit, pp. 24-35.

Pianificazione e Disegno delle Università (Italy), by Giancarlo De Carlo, 1968: Tougaloo College, pp. 93-98.

Architectural Forum, January-February 1969: "Federal Reserve in Suspense," pp. 100-105.

Deutsche Bauzeitung (Germany), February 1969, no. 2: Tougaloo College, Mississippi, p. 116.

Progressive Architecture, April 1969: "No Space for the Cultural Square" (Livonia Public Library, Livonia, Michigan), pp. 146-149.

Detroit Free Press, May 11, 1969: "Detroit's Ten Best Buildings," p. 9.

Baumeister 7 (Germany), B1547E, July 1969: "Brückgurt-Fassade" (Federal Reserve Bank of Minneapolis), p. 847.

Kenchiku Bunka (Japan), vol. 24, no. 275, September 1969: Federal Reserve Bank of Minneapolis, pp. 79-82.

Domus (Italy), October 1969, no. 479: Federal Reserve Bank of Minneapolis, p. 1.

Arkitekten (Denmark), 1969, no. 19: "Bankbygning i Minneapolis," pp. 810-812.

L'Architecture d'Aujourd'hui (France), October-November 1969, no. 146: "Banque Fédérale à Minneapolis," pp. xix, xx.

Architecture & Planning 6 (Taiwan), November 1969: "Gunnar Birkerts–Architect," pp. 43-51.

Deutsche Bauzeitung (Germany), 1969, no. 11: "Bankprojekt in Minnesota," pp. 789-792.

Kenchiku Bunka 3 (Japan), March 1970, vol. 25, no. 281: "Gunnar Birkerts" (Lincoln Elementary School; Livonia Public Library; Glen Oaks Community College; Fisher Administrative Building, University of Detroit; Tougaloo College), pp. 139-158.

Werk (Switzerland), no. 4, 1970: "Eine Brücke' für die Federal Reserve Bank in Minneapolis," p. 211.

Baumeister 5 (Germany), May 1970: "Kettenlinie und Bogen" (Federal Reserve Bank of Minneapolis), pp. 524-526.

Casabella (Italy), May 1970, no. 348: "University Versus City," p. 10.

The Art Gallery, May 1970: Contemporary Arts Museum, Houston, pp. 19-21.

Architectural Forum, November 1970: "Academic Village" (Dance Instructional Facility, State University, Purchase, New York), pp. 35-40.

Deutsche Bauzeitung 12 (Germany), 1970: "Den Kreis durchbrochen" (Corning Library, New York), p. 1094.

Baumeister 12 (Germany), December 1970: "Bücher–Brücke" (Corning Library, New York), p. 1461.

L'Architettura (Italy), May 1971: "Opere e progetti di Gunnar Birkerts e Associati," pp. 34-42.

Progressive Architecture, January 1971: Design Awards Program, IBM Computer Facility, Sterling Forest, New York, pp. 88-89.

Arkitekten (Denmark), no. 9, 1971: "To Amerikanske Biblioteksprosekter" (Corning Library; Duluth Public Library), pp. A334-A338.

Architectural Record, October 1971: "New Directions for Gunnar Birkerts," pp. 97-110.

Architectural Forum, November 1971: "Subterranean Systems," pp. 58-59.

Baumeister (Germany), December 1971: "Computer Center bei New York," pp. 1542-1543.

Architecture & Urbanism (Japan), July 1972: Special Issue on Gunnar Birkerts.

Popular Science, August 1972: "This Building Is a Bridge" (Federal Reserve Bank, Minneapolis), pp. 64-65.

Bâtir (France), September 1972: Federal Reserve Bank of Minneapolis, pp. 3-6.

Art in America, September-October 1972: Contemporary Arts Museum, Houston, pp. 50-51.

Stern (Germany), November 1972: Federal Reserve Bank of Minneapolis, pp. 246, 248.

Progressive Architecture, December 1972: "Machines in Sterling Forest–IBM Information Center," pp. 50-55.

Fortune, February 1973: "Sleek Skins and Structural Bones" (Federal Reserve Bank of Minneapolis), p. 86.

Progressive Architecture, March 1973: "Liberating Land," Subterranean Study, pp. 73-79.

Acier-Stahl-Steel (Belgium), June 1973: "Suspended Bank Building: Federal Reserve Bank at Minneapolis (U.S.A.)," pp. 250-255.

Span (USIA), October 1973: "New American Architecture," p. 46.

Architectural Record, November 1973: "The Federal Reserve Bank of Minneapolis and Dormitory and Library Buildings for Tougaloo College," pp. 105-116.

The Kentiku (Japan), December 1973: "Gunnar Birkerts," pp. 51-92.

Domus (Italy), December 1973: "Computer sul lago" (IBM Computer Center), pp. 29-32.

Northwest Architect, January-February 1974: "The Bank's Bank," pp. 4-7, 33-35.

Civil Engineering, April 1974: "Eleven Projects Nominated for 1974 Achievement Award" (Federal Reserve Bank of Minneapolis), p. 78.

Trends 16 (Japan), Contemporary Arts Museum, Houston, pp. 34, 35.

L'Espresso (Italy), March 24, 1974: "Il mondo visto da una banca," by Bruno Zevi, pp. 68-69.

The Canadian Architect, June 1974: "Design: 'The Critical Years,' Subterranean Systems," pp. 48-52.

Space Design (Japan), August 1974: "Federal Reserve Bank of Minneapolis," pp. 5-39.

Architecture & Urbanism (Japan), September 1974: "Federal Reserve Bank of Minneapolis - USA," pp. 35-66.

Domus (Italy), January 1975: "A Minneapolis la banca" (Federal Reserve Bank of Minneapolis), p. 18.

Progressive Architecture, March 1975: "Varied Reflections in Houston" (Contemporary Arts Museum), pp. 52-57.

Space Design (Japan), September 1975: Contemporary Arts Museum, Houston; Fire Station, Corning, New York; Visitor Reception Center, Dearborn, Michigan, pp. 52-64.

Progressive Architecture, September 1975: "By Reflected Light - Office Building, Detroit" (IBM Office Building, Southfield, Michigan), pp. 58-63.

Domus (Italy), July 1976: Contemporary Arts Museum, Houston; Fire Station, Corning, New York; IBM Office Building, Southfield, Michigan, pp. 17-21.

Bouwwereld (Netherlands), August 1976: Federal Reserve Bank of Minneapolis, pp. 14-17.

Architecture & Urbanism (Japan), October 1976: "Gunnar Birkerts" (Fire Station, Corning, N.Y.; Calvary Baptist Church; Visitor Reception Center; Dual Mode Transit System), pp. 68-88.

Nikkei Architecture (Japan), October 4, 1976: "Leading Architects of the World: Gunnar Birkerts," pp. 48-50.

Engineering News-Record, February 10, 1977: "Architect Clads Michigan Office Tower with Energy Conserving Wall" (IBM Office Building, Southfield, Michigan), p. 13.

Architectural Record, February 1977: "A School for the Dance by Gunnar Birkerts," pp. 85-94.

Progressive Architecture, March 1977: "Two Machines" (Fire Station, Corning, New York), pp. 58-61.

Progressive Architecture, April 1977: "On Alvar Aalto," by Gunnar Birkerts, pp. 54-55.

Popular Science, June 1977: "Energy-saving Wall" (IBM Office Building, Southfield, Michigan), p. 73.

L'Architettura (Italy), November 1977: Dance Instructional Facility, State University, Purchase, New York, pp. 390-391.

The Christian Science Monitor, December 15, 1977: "Architecture–The Impetus to Build," pp. 27-29.

The Japan Architect, A View of Contemporary World Architects, December 1977: "Gunnar Birkerts–Federal Reserve Bank of Minneapolis," pp. 61, 93.

Space Design (Japan), February 1978: "Dance Instructional Facility," pp. 5-12.

Saudi Gazette (Saudi Arabia), March 2, 1978: "Architect Who Puts Poetry into His Buildings," p. 5.

Architecture & Urbanism (Japan), July 1978: "Dance Instructional Facility," pp. 39-46.

Architecture & Urbanism (Japan), October 1978: "The Calvary Baptist Church," Detroit, Michigan, pp. 49-54.

(Selected Bibliography)

Building Design & Construction, January 1979: "Systems & Technology" (IBM Office Building, Southfield, Michigan), pp. 40-47.

Decade, February 1979: "Metaphor in Design," pp. 13-17.

Dichotomy (University of Detroit), April 1979: "The Philosophy and Methodology of Gunnar Birkerts: Current Thoughts," pp. 10-12.

Civil Engineering, May 1979: "Underground Buildings: Energy Savers?" (University of Michigan Law Library Addition), p. 85.

Architectural Record, October 1979: "Two New Energy Sources" (IBM Office Building, Southfield, Michigan; Calvary Baptist Church, Detroit), pp. 87-96.

The Christian Science Monitor, November 9, 1979: "Let's 'Bank' Energy Savings in Buildings" (IBM Office Building, Southfield, Michigan), p. 19.

Today's Structural Designer in U.S.A., by Shigeru Mochizuki (Japan), fall 1979: Federal Reserve Bank in Minneapolis, pp. 20-23, 194-195.

Time, December 24, 1979: "The Cooling of America" (IBM Office Building, Southfield, Michigan), p. 56.

Newsweek, April 7, 1980: "The Solar Revolution" (IBM Office Building, Southfield, Michigan), pp. 79-85.

Smithsonian, May 1980: "A New Glass House to House the Best of Beautiful Glass" (Corning Museum of Glass), pp. 66-76.

New York Times Magazine, June 1, 1980: "Splendor in the Glass Museum" (Corning Museum of Glass), pp. 76, 77.

The Washington Post, June 7, 1980: "Splendor in the Glass" (Corning Museum of Glass).

Time, June 30, 1980: "A New Museum for an Ancient Art" (Corning Museum of Glass), pp. 63-64.

Americana, July-August 1980: "After the Flood" (Corning Museum of Glass), pp. 20-23.

Industrial Design, July-August 1980: "Corning Museum and Exhibits – A First Critique," pp. 36-41.

Progressive Architecture, July 1980: Corning Museum of Glass, p. 25.

American Way, October 1980: "A Museum Built on Sand" (Corning Museum of Glass), pp. 126-133.

Architectural Record, November 1980: "Birkerts' Library for Duluth," pp. 86-91.

GA Document (Japan), Special Issue 1970-1980, fall 1980: Federal Reserve Bank of Minneapolis, pp. 68-69.

GA Document No. 2 (Japan), fall 1980: Duluth Public Library and Corning Museum of Glass, pp. 92-107.

Inland Architect, November 1980: "The Long Baltic Current," pp. 6-17.

Dichotomy (University of Detroit), fall 1980: "Gunnar Birkerts: A Steady Influence in a City of Turmoil," pp. 3-5.

Architectural Record, February 1981: "Reflections on a Glass Museum" (Corning Museum of Glass), pp. 67-73.

Nikkei Architecture (Japan), March 1981: Duluth Public Library, pp. 80-83.

Space Design (Japan), April 1981: "Three Recent Works of Gunnar Birkerts" (Corning Museum of Glass; Duluth Public Library; Calvary Baptist Church), pp. 3-20.

Inland Architect, May 1981: "The Eero Saarinen Spawn," p. 37.

AIA Journal, Mid-May 1981: "Shining and Sinuous Structure" (Corning Museum of Glass, New York), pp. 182-191.

America Illustrated (Moscow), August 1981: Duluth Public Library, pp. 23-25.

Techniques & Architecture (France), September 1981: IBM Office Building, Southfield, Michigan, pp. 72-73.

L'Architettura (Italy), September 1981: Corning Museum of Glass; Calvary Baptist Church; IBM Office Building, Southfield, Michigan; Duluth Public Library; pp. 502-520.

Domus (Italy), October 1981: "Linear Periscope" (Corning Museum of Glass), pp. 22-25.

Architectural Record, March 1982: "Architecture beneath the Surface" (University of Michigan Law Library Addition), pp. 77-85.

The Buildings Journal, May 17, 1982: List of Top Ten Architects, p. 12.

Architecture & Urbanism (Japan), July 1982: "University of Michigan Law Library Addition and Woodbranch Energy Plaza Four Project," pp. 21-36.

The Architects Journal (England), July 28, 1982: "Underground Books" (University of Michigan Law Library Addition), pp. 24-33.

L'Architettura (Italy), August-September 1982: University of Michigan Law Library Addition, pp. 590-595.

Domus (Italy), September 1982, no. 631: "Underground Landscape" (University of Michigan Law Library Addition), pp. 22-23.

AIA Journal, January 1983: "'Splendor Beneath the Grass' in Michigan" (University of Michigan Law Library Addition), pp. 50-55.

Space Design (Japan), February 1983, no. 221: "Space Design for Energy Conservation in America, District Office Building/State of Wisconsin," pp. 17-20.

Architectural Record, March 1983: "Explorations: Four Projects by Gunnar Birkerts," pp. 108-113.

L'Industria delle Costruzioni (Italy), May 1983, no. 139: "Facoltà di Legge dell'Università del Michigan" (University of Michigan Law Library Addition), pp. 46-53.

Architecture & Urbanism (Japan), Extra Edition: Alvar Aalto, May 1983: "Aalto's Design Methodology," by Gunnar Birkerts, pp. 13-14.

Montana State Architectural Review, vol. 1, spring 1983: "Aalto – Vuoksenniska and the Modern Movement," by Gunnar Birkerts, pp. 10-11.

Reflections (The Journal of the School of Architecture, University of Illinois at Urbana-Champaign), vol. 1, no. 1, fall 1983: "Gunnar Birkerts Interviewed by G.B.," pp. 12-15.

Baumeister (Germany), November 1983, no. 11: "Erweiterung der Universitätsbibliothek" (University of Michigan Law Library Addition), pp. 1063-1067.

The Globe and Mail, December 10, 1983: "One Creative Mind That Plays with a Full Deck," by Adele Freedman, p. 15.

L'Architettura (Italy), December 1983, no. 338: "Biblioteca della Cornell University a Ithaca, New York," pp. 864-868.

Underground Space, vol. 8, 1984: "Harnessing the Nineteenth Century: Subterranean Urban Systems," by Gunnar Birkerts, pp. 44-51.

GA Document No. 9 (Japan), February 1984: College of Law, University of Iowa, pp. 96-99.

Architecture & Urbanism (Japan), Extra Edition: Eero Saarinen, April 1984: "Interviewee-3, Gunnar Birkerts," pp. 223-225.

GA Houses 16 (Japan), July 1984: "Villa Ginny," pp. 122-129.

Domus (Italy), July-August 1984, no. 652: "Villa Ginny," pp. 34-39.

L'Architettura (Italy), December 1984: "Recent Realizations by Gunnar Birkerts and Associates" (District Office Building, Green Bay, Wisconsin; Baldwin Public Library Addition, Birmingham, Michigan; Chapel and Educational Facility, Camp Wildflecken, Germany), pp. 876-888.

Architecture & Urbanism (Japan), March 1985: "11 Works of Gunnar Birkerts and Associates Architects" (U.S. Embassy Office Building, Helsinki, Finland; District Office Building, Green Bay, Wisconsin; Citrin Office Building, Bingham Farms, Michigan; Bus Shelter, Corning Museum of Glass, Corning, New York; Chapel & Educational Facility, Camp Wildflecken, Germany; Unity of The Infinite Presence, Warren, Michigan; Muiznieks Residence, Kalamazoo, Michigan; Wick Alumni Center, Lincoln, Nebraska; Headquarters Library Competition, Anchorage, Alaska; Ferguson Residence, Kalamazoo, Michigan; Uris Library Addition, Cornell University), pp. 11-18.

Baumeister (Germany), April 1985: "Bibliothek in Ithaca, USA" (Uris Library Addition, Cornell University), pp. 68-70.

Architecture & Urbanism (Japan), July 1985: "Ferguson Residence, Kalamazoo, Michigan," pp. 25-30.

A Style for the Year 2001, JA/A+U Joint Extra Edition (Japan), summer 1985: "Gunnar Birkerts" (College of Law, University of Iowa; Domino's Farms, Ann Arbor, Michigan), pp. 78-79.

Architecture In Greece (Greece), no. 19, 1985: "Gunnar Birkerts and Associates, Architects" (University of Michigan Law Library Addition; IBM Office Building, Southfield, Michigan; Duluth Public Library; Federal Reserve Bank of Minneapolis; Museum of Glass, Corning, New York; IBM Corporate Computer Center, Sterling Forest, New York; Lincoln Elementary School, Columbus, Indiana; Dance Instructional Facility, State University, Purchase, New York), pp. 102-104.

Faith & Form, fall 1985: "The Design of a Chapel Facility," by Gunnar Birkerts (Chapel and Educational Facility, Camp Wildflecken, Germany), pp. 32-34.

Architecture & Urbanism (Japan), December 1985: "Cornell University, Uris Undergraduate Library Addition," and "Camp Wildflecken/Chapel and Education Facility," pp. 91-100.

Inland Architect, January-February 1986: "Gunnar Birkerts and the Domino Theory," by Robert Benson, pp. 20-27, and "An Interview with Gunnar Birkerts," pp. 28-33.

Architecture, February 1986: "Library Addition Inserted into a Hill" (Uris Library Addition, Cornell University), pp. 50-53.

L'Architettura (Italy), March 1986: "G. Birkerts and Associates: Ferguson Residence a Kalamazoo, Michigan," pp. 204-205.

Iowa Architect, September-October 1986: "College of Law, University of Iowa, Iowa City," pp. 20-23.

(Selected Bibliography)

The San Diego Union, December 14, 1986: "Birkerts Wears Proudly the Mantle of Modernism," by Kay Kaiser, p. F-2.

Architecture, December 1986: "A Very, Very Long Version of a Prairie House" (Domino's Farms, Ann Arbor, Michigan), pp. 62-65.

Detail (Germany), January-February 1987: "Erweiterung der Uris Bibliothek" (Cornell University in Ithaca, New York, Uris Library Addition), Tafel I-III.

Architectural Record, March 1987: "Formed to Light: Thirteen Projects by Gunnar Birkerts" (Albion Church, Albion, Michigan; University Reformed Church, Ann Arbor, Michigan; Freeman Residence, Grand Rapids, Michigan; Ferguson Residence, Kalamazoo, Michigan; Lincoln Elementary School, Columbus, Indiana; Dance Instruction Facility, State University, Purchase; Law School Addition, University of Michigan, Ann Arbor; Duluth Public Library, Minnesota; College of Law Building, University of Iowa, Iowa City; Anchorage Library Competition, Alaska; IBM Office Building, Southfield, Michigan; Citrin Office Building, Bingham Farms, Michigan; Museum of Glass, Corning, New York), pp. 140-149.

L'Architettura (Italy), March 1987: "Domino's Pizza: uffici-fattoria ad Ann Arbor, Michigan, Architetto Gunnar Birkerts," pp. 190-202.

Architecture & Urbanism (Japan), April 1987, no. 199: "Domino's Farms World Headquarters, Ann Arbor, Michigan," and "College of Law Building, University of Iowa, Iowa City," pp. 73-88.

Detail (Germany), May-June 1987: "Uris Bibliothek, Cornell University in Ithaca, New York, Uris Library," pp. 245-248.

Glass Today (Report on the proceedings of The Glass In The Environment Conference, London, April 1986; edited by Michael Wigginton, published by the Crafts Council), "Poetry and Metaphor in Building Design," by Gunnar Birkerts, pp. 16-19.

Baumeister (Germany), August 1987: "College of Law In Iowa City, USA," pp. 32-33.

Architectural Record, August 1987: "The University of Iowa/College of Law, Iowa City, Iowa," pp. 106-113.

Faith & Form, fall 1987: "Looking for Michelangelo and Finding Bernini" (Cathedral of the Most Blessed Sacrament, Detroit, Michigan), pp. 35-38.

L'Arca (Italy), October 1987: "The Artificial Cavern" (Law School Addition, University of Michigan, Ann Arbor; Uris Library Addition, Cornell University, Ithaca, New York), pp. 32-43.

L'Architettura (Italy), December 1987: "Facoltà di Giurisprudenza dell'Università dell'Iowa a Iowa City" (University of Iowa College of Law), pp. 854-865.

L'Espresso (Italy), January 31, 1988: "Un omaggio pendente," by Bruno Zevi (Domino's Farms Tower, Ann Arbor, Michigan).

Maksla (Latvia), April 1988: Gunars Birkerts: Turpinajums," pp. 20-25.

The New York Times, May 1, 1988: "A Pizza Empire Strives for the Wright Stuff," by Paul Goldberger (Domino's Farms, Michigan), p. 36.

The Ann Arbor News, May 29, 1988: "Don't Box Him In," by Katherine Blair, pp. D1-D2.

L'Arca (Italy), July-August 1988: "Papal Thrones" and "Inside Detroit Stadium" (Papal Altar and Furniture), pp. 44-49.

Techniques & Architecture (France), August-September 1988, no. 379: "Sur la prairie" (Domino's Farms, Ann Arbor, Michigan), pp. 128-133.

L'Arca (Italy), September 1988, no. 19: "Domino's Tower, Rural High Rise" (Domino's Farms, Ann Arbor, Michigan), pp. 16-23.

L'Industria delle Costruzioni (Italy), September 1988: "Facoltà di Giurisprudenza dell'Università dello Iowa" (University of Iowa College of Law, Iowa City), pp. 20-29.

Ottagono (Italy), September 1988: "An Architectural Piece for Fourteen Hands" (Program Spa [Fiat], Florence), pp. 52-57.

Inland Architect, September-October 1988: "Michigan Politicians Look Up From Down Under" (Preservation Master Plan, Michigan State Capitol), pp. 13, 16.

L'Architettura (Italy), October 1988: "Chiesa luterana di St. Peter a Columbus, Indiana" (St. Peter's Lutheran Church, Columbus, Indiana), pp. 702-712.

Faith & Form, winter 1988-89: "Another Jewel in the Crown: St. Peter's Lutheran Church, Columbus, Indiana," by Kay Kaiser, pp. 9-13.

Credits

Partners and Senior Associates
(1959 - Present)
Frank Straub
Barbara Bos
Charles Fleckenstein
John Hilberry
Almon Durkee
Vytautas Usas
Harold Van Dine
Gunars Ejups
Anthony Gholz
Kenneth Rohlfing

Associates in the Firm
(1959 - Present)
Robert Bodnar
Keith Brown
David Chasco
Daniel Dennison
Russell Dixon
Anthony Duce
Anthony Foust
Kenneth Kemp
Keiichi Miyashita
Richard Pavlichek
Kathleen Reehil
Edward Rosella
Kevin Shultis
Mary Jane Williamson
William Wolfe

Current and Past Assistants
(1959 - Present)
Diane Acciaioli
Richard Adelson
William Ahlstrom
Donald Altemeyer
Moiz Anandwala
Thomas Andreoli
Mark Attwood
Katherine Austin
William Awodey
Clifton Balch
Mojdeh Baratloo
Francis Bartlett
Dian Bauer
Vija Berzins
Andra Birkerts
Sven Birkerts
Alan Black
Kay (Heinzerling) Block
Robert Bodnar
Stanley Boles
Richard Borrelli
Richard Bos
Robert Brown
Susan Brozes
William Bruder
Michael Bruner
Algimantas Bublys
Janet Burke
Richard Burt
Mary Butler
Gary Calley
Mary Campbell
Paul Canvasser
Judi Capen
Gordon Carrier
Donna Christman
Eduardo Gascon Climent
Jack Cross

Jeffrey Crowell
Patrick Czeski
Gary Desmond
Paul DesRochers
Peter Dobrovolny
James Dome
Joseph Druffel
Joseph Dudas
Edward Durant
George Emmert
Mark Farlow
Joe Filip
Michael Filipowicz
Richard Fredrikson
Bruno Fuciarelli
Richard Fuher
Frederick Furr
Emily Galusha
Louis Gauci
Hyman Gittleman
Frederic Glade
Page Goode
Jane Graham
Laverne Greely
Paul Greene
Janice Greer
George (Fritz) Grohs
Bryan Gross
Jacob Guter
Henry Guthard
Bart Guthrie
Chris Hanson
Thomas Hansz
Patrick Harris
Mark Harsha
William Hartman
Helen Hawtin
Charles Held
John Hinkley
Kent Hubbell
Suzanne Hughes
Jun Ikawa
Marlene Imirzian
Fred John
Abraham Kadushin
Dagmar Kaiser
Robert Kalvar
Dharam Kambo
Steven Kelly
Kenneth Killian
Glenn Klosterhaus
Philip Klump
Taher Koita
Richard Lacombe
John Landry
Jack Lee
Paul Chu Lin
Lynn Loebl
Robert Lynch
Chris Matthesius
Timothy McKay
John Miller
Judy Miller
George Mitton
Marina Montemayor
Makito Mori
Ayers Morison
Katsuya Morita
Hal Moseley
John Mueller
Edmund Narbutas
Theodore Nolte
William Nowysz
Jeffrey Ochsner
Randall Ott

Dennis Page
Jeffrey Pedersen
Michael Pernack
Lillian Peterson
Armands Petersons
Kent Pool
Frederick Porter
Thomas Ray
Renate Reimer
John Reuter
Ralph Rhoads
Donald Root
Edward Rosella
Manfred Sabatke
James Sauer
Bridget Schulze
John Schwartz
Karen Siefert
Joseph Slajus
Andrejs Smiltars
Craig Smith
Linda Smith
Clifford Snyder
Halyna Sobkiw
John Sparks
Francis Stanisz
Mark Steele
Jack Stephens
Dana Stimson
William Stuart
Harry Svendblad
Ian Taberner
Mits Takayama
William Tazelaar
Leslie Thomas
Ahmet Tukel
Tim Van Dusen
Dave Van Horn
Joseph Vargo
Bruce Wade
Donald Wenderski
James Williamson
Clyde Wilson
Lloyd Wright
Abraham Yolles
Todd Young
Robert Zalbrowski
Suzanne Zukowski

Structural Engineers

Robert Darvas
Clifford Holforty
Nickifor Lebar
William LeMessurier
Leslie Robertson

Photography credits
Robert Chase:
Page 208

Balthazar Korab:
Pages 31, 34, 36, 37, 38, 39, 40,
41, 45, 59, 60, 61, 62, 63, 64,
65, 70, 71, 74, 75, 76, 77, 80,
82, 95, 107, 131, 142, 155, 184, 185

Balthazar Korab Ltd.:
Pages 90, 91, 92, 93, 101, 103,
105, 106

Timothy Hursley:
Pages 87, 112, 113, 114, 115,
119, 122, 123, cover

Keiichi Miyashita:
Pages 32, 33, 35, 43, 44, 46, 47,
49, 50, 51, 55, 57, 66, 67, 117,
125, 126, 127, 128, 144, 150,
157, 158, 161, 163, 164, 165,
166, 171, 181, 182, 195, 197,
202, 203, 205, 206

Hedrich Blessing:
Page 53

Joseph Molitor:
Page 79

Ed Stewart:
Page 135

John Williams (PWB):
Page 142, lower right

Mike Rebholz:
Page 129

Gunnar Birkerts:
Page 81

Paul Chu Lin:
Pages 84, 85, 86

University of Iowa:
Pages 111, 112, upper left

Illustration courtesy of City of
Lansing, Michigan, Planning
Division:
Page 200